A Clean Camel is a Happy Camel

A
Clean Camel
is a
Happy Camel

Written by
Paul Symonds

Illustrated by
Mark Shotter

First published by O Books, 2007
O Books is an imprint of John Hunt Publishing Ltd., The Bothy, Deershot Lodge, Park Lane, Ropley, Hants, SO24 0BE, UK
office1@o-books.net
www.o-books.net

Distribution in:

UK and Europe
Orca Book Services
orders@orcabookservices.co.uk
Tel: 01202 665432 Fax: 01202 666219 Int. code (44)

USA and Canada
NBN
custserv@nbnbooks.com
Tel: 1 800 462 6420 Fax: 1 800 338 4550

Australia and New Zealand
Brumby Books
sales@brumbybooks.com.au
Tel: 61 3 9761 5535 Fax: 61 3 9761 7095

Far East (offices in Singapore, Thailand, Hong Kong, Taiwan)
Pansing Distribution Pte Ltd
kemal@pansing.com
Tel: 65 6319 9939 Fax: 65 6462 5761

South Africa
Alternative Books
altbook@peterhyde.co.za
Tel: 021 447 5300 Fax: 021 447 1430

Text copyright Paul Symonds 2007

Design: Mark Shotter

ISBN-13: 978 1 84694 036 1
ISBN-10: 1 84694 036 2

A CIP catalogue record for this book is available from the British Library.

Printed in the UK by Ashford Press

Acknowledgements

There are a few people I'd like to thank for helping me in the creation of this book – and these are in no particular order.

My wife, Michelle, had the foresight to go out and get a proper job when we first got married, thus allowing me to stay at home and write. Although I do now have a job, without that time to write, I wouldn't have had half of the ideas for this book and it probably would never have happened.

I'm very grateful to Mark Shotter for spurning his university education – and, by extension, his entire future – in order to illustrate this book. You'll have a mansion in heaven, Mark. He and Jonathan Abdy have also each contributed a cartoon idea or two – so thanks for that.

I'm also very grateful to Trevor Shotter, both for his encouragement and his advice throughout the writing of this book. Trevor, you laughed when others only looked puzzled.

A big 'thank you' as well to Michael Wescott and Dave Helm for making it possible for me to see an early version of the book in print (especially Michael, who discussed the book at length with me over numerous chicken stir-fries).

And finally, thank you, Tasha McNaught, for creating the original cover.

Paul Symonds

Introduction

The Bible has been around for a while now and most people know something about Jesus' life, either from reading the Gospels or learning the stories at Sunday School. The Three Wise Men, for instance, or Jesus walking on water, John the Baptist losing his head, the Triumphal Entry or the Ascension into heaven are all well known to many of us. But there are many important questions that are left unanswered about these events. What did the three wise men do *before* they were wise? How did Jesus' ability to walk on water affect the lifesaving profession? Was it hygienic to bring a severed head so close to food? Whose job was it to pick up all the palm leaves once Jesus had triumphantly entered Jerusalem? And what would innocent passers-by have made of Jesus floating up to heaven?

All these questions and many more that you have probably never asked are answered in this book, because, for the first time in nearly two thousand years, the research material used by Luke to write his gospel (you can't miss it – it's the third one – cunningly entitled 'The Gospel According To Luke') has been gathered together.

Never again will you wonder what colour the disciples painted the Upper Room or what John the Baptist liked to eat with his locusts or even how to go about buying your first camel. It's all answered here in this jolly useful little book. Enjoy.

Dr. Luke Ben Jahash PhD, KJV, NASB, NIV
Physician and Divine Biographer

To: Theophilus
37a Broad Street
Rome

My Dear Theophilus,

Thanks so much for your comments regarding the account of Jesus' life I sent you. They were very encouraging, I must say. Do you really think I could get it published? It's hard to tell if it's any good, as the only other person to have read it is my mother, who thinks it's wonderful – but she thinks everything I do is wonderful. There was this time when I was eleven and we all had to make something for the school assembly – but you're probably not interested in that.

I've put all my research material together like you asked and I'm sending them along with this letter. It took some doing, gathering it all, I can tell you. There are some confidential Sanhedrin documents included and some of the material is quite old now. I didn't use everything I collected, as you'll see, but it's all useful background stuff.

My, this is all very exciting, isn't it? Maybe I should get started on a sequel – I could call it 'The Amazing Adventures of the Apostles'. What do you think? Well, maybe I'm getting a bit ahead of myself. First things first, eh? I hope this is useful, and I'll see you at the Pulitzer Prize winners' party.

Your good friend,

Luke

Paradise Lost!

Reports are just coming in that the first and greatest calamity of all history has occurred only weeks after history itself began.

Details are sketchy, but we believe Adam and Eve - the first humans to set foot on the earth – have openly defied the only restriction God placed on their stay in the much-sought-after Garden of Eden.

God had given Adam and Eve free reign of the fruits of all the trees of the Garden, with the one exception of the Tree of the Knowledge of Good and Evil. However, following a brief discussion with an, as yet, unidentified reptile, it appears both Adam *and* Eve ate from the tree's fruit. As a direct result of this trespass, they have both been banished from the Garden of Eden for an indefinite period, though we believe they are planning on appealing.

Although, on the face of it, this may seem a relatively small transgression, the results of the couple's action are much more far-reaching than they could have imagined. According to our sources, mankind will no longer be able to live in harmony with God, which almost certainly means an ever widening chasm will develop between creation and Creator, resulting in war, famine, disease,

earthquakes, floods, plagues, mushrooms, pestilence, death and, of course, eternal separation from God.

The couple have released a statement to the press, which reads simply, *'Oops!'*.

In a slightly lengthier statement, God had this to say about the incident:

'I am obviously deeply saddened by the actions of my two favourite creations. The snake that tempted them to eat the apple has been severely punished and, I'm afraid, Adam and Eve and all that come after them must also reap the consequences.

It is true that there is now a chasm separating mankind and myself, but I can assure you that this is not the end. I am even now working on a plan to undo the considerable damage done here this week.

I cannot reveal any details at this point but watch this space.'

Dear All,

Well, another year is over and it's time for my annual look back over the past few months. It's been a busy old time, all in all, what with the halo-tossing championships last month (well done, Nathan) and the unveiling of yet another selection of psalms by David last summer – I believe that makes 69,345 psalms altogether now. Keep it up, Dave; you're doing a grand job! And let's not forget what's been going on down on earth. The Romans have been invading ever more countries and the barbarians are going wild up in the north (it's what they do best, after all) - and lets not forget my chosen people, bless 'em. I sometimes wonder if they'll ever understand what following me is all about. Which brings me to some important news.

As you are all aware, there has been, for many years now, a problem down on earth – and I don't mean the smell problem (you'll be pleased to know I've decided to get the Romans to invent the bath) – I mean the sin problem.

Ever since Adam and Eve ate that apple, there's been no end of trouble down there. I've tried all sorts to make things right: sacrifices, promises, great escapes – you name it, I've tried it. We need something new – and I've come up with a solution that will end the sin problem for good. I have decided to go to earth myself.

Now, just in case you were thinking that if someone saw the eternal God, Creator and Lord of the universe, walking around Israel, it might strike them as being somewhat odd, I've already thought of that. I am going to go in disguise. In fact, I am going to go in the form of a Yucca Plant.

Just kidding.

I am, in fact, going to go disguised as a plain, ordinary human being. And not only that but I am going to have to be killed. This is, I'm afraid, the only way to save the human race from hell. No matter how good they try to be, it's just not enough. They'll never reach perfection on their own. So I'm going to do it for them.

The more shrewd among you may have noticed a potential flaw to this plan – how can I keep the universe and everything in it going if I become a part of it? Well, I've thought of that too. I will remain here in heaven as Sovereign over all creation, but I will also be down on earth in the form of my Son and this human form will be filled with my Spirit, so whoever follows him will also be following me. And if you didn't quite follow all that, that's because it's a mystery – and a doozy at that! I think I'll call it 'The Trinity' – it'll keep the theologians busy for centuries.

All that's left to do now is to let people down there know what's happening. Gabriel's got a few announcements to make and Raphael is, as we speak, organising a party, the likes of which you have never seen – and you're all invited!

See you there!

God

Speechless!

There was an unusual disturbance at the temple last night involving one of the evening staff. Zechariah, the priest on duty, is reported to have been struck dumb whilst working in the sanctuary. Other priests have verified that the veteran temple worker was definitely speaking yesterday morning when he began his duties but that he was unable to utter a single word when he left for home in the evening.

According to neighbours' reports, Zechariah was seen motioning wildly with his hands at his wife, Elizabeth, who eventually fell to the floor with a short scream. A neighbour called the police but by the time they arrived, Elizabeth was up and about and smiling.

She explained to the police that her husband had received a vision in the temple wherein the Angel Gabriel had told him that his wife, aged 57, was going to have a baby boy.

The couple had apparently been trying for a baby for many years before finally giving up hope and Elizabeth has described her feelings as 'shocked but delighted'.

She further explained that 'the silly old fool wouldn't believe the angel, so he was struck dumb until the baby arrives.'

As nobody was in the temple with Zechariah, it is difficult to corroborate the priest's story. Temple officials are, however, looking into it.

Zechariah made no comment.

Letting It All Hang Out!

Thrill seekers in Rome yesterday got more than they bargained for when a young man ran naked across the Coliseum stage during a gladiator fight. The streaker (name unknown) managed to dodge several Roman soldiers and one or two gladiators, before being caught in a net.

Much to the disappointment of the crowd, Caesar gave the man the 'thumbs down' and he was taken off to be eaten by the big cats in the second half.

When asked why he had done it, the man replied, 'My mate down the tavern bet me 10 sestertii I wouldn't do it. I'll be round to pick up my winnings as soon as these guards have shown me their cats.'

Unfortunately for the streaker, the cats in the second half were slightly bigger and hungrier than he had anticipated and the friend in question got away without paying up.

SEE THE
PICTURES ON
PAGE 3!

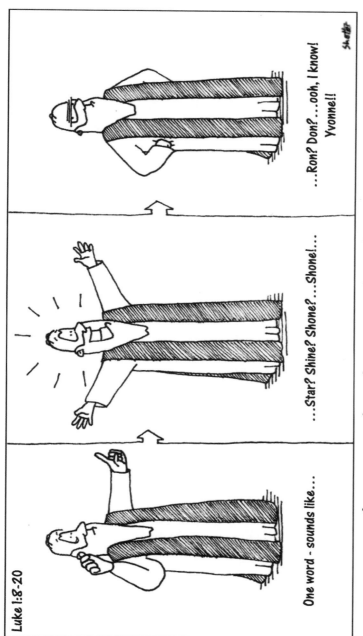

Amongst other things, Zechariah is credited with inventing Charades

Dear Aunt Belinda

Dear Aunt Belinda,

I am a 14 year-old boy and I am writing to you because I have an embarrassing problem. I've got spots all over my face and my back. I know a lot of people my age get spots, but mine are really bad. All the kids at school call me Leper Face and last week, some of them gave me a bell to ring, saying I was unclean. I've tried lots of different oils but nothing seems to work. What do you suggest?

Spotty of Caesarea

Aunt Belinda writes...

Dear Spotty,

Spots can be a big problem for boys your age. Just when you're beginning to think about girls in a new way, I expect they're finding you repulsive and wouldn't dream of kissing you. But don't worry; our law is very clear about what to do in these cases – and it couldn't be simpler. Just go to a priest in Jerusalem and show him your spots, he'll examine them and then put you in isolation for a week. If they've gone by the end of the week, you're free to go, and those girls won't know what hit them. If, however, your spots are still there, you must stay in isolation for another week. This process goes on either until you get better or the priest decides you have an infectious disease – though I'm sure that won't happen in your case - but don't throw that bell away just yet.

Dear Aunt Belinda,

I am a thirteen year-old boy and I've got a big problem. My mum and dad bought me a pet camel for my bar mitzvah, which was great because I've always wanted a camel - even from when I was young. The trouble is, now my parents won't let me practise racing it in the house. I can't go outside, otherwise Moses (my camel) would get dirty and then I'd have to wash him, but my mum says she doesn't want camel prints all over her newly washed floors. I think they're being selfish and unreasonable. Can you help me?

Persecuted of Bethany

Aunt Belinda writes...

Dear Persecuted,

I can see from your letter that you are very distressed by this whole 'camel in the house' issue. Have you, I wonder, considered the fact that you might be a spoilt little brat who thinks the world revolves around him? I think the best advice I can give you is to ask your dad to give you a good thrashing and then get him to send you out at 5:00 every morning to clean and water your poor camel, Moses. I hope that was some help.

Dear Aunt Belinda,

I am a sixteen year-old girl from Nazareth and I am writing to you because I'm having a bit of trouble with my fiancé. We were promised to each other about six months ago and everything was fine, but then something a bit unusual happened. One day, while I was working at home on my own, I was visited by the Angel Gabriel. He seemed very nice and we were chatting about the wedding and everything – he gave me some lovely tips for the dress – when all of a sudden he sort of mentioned that I was going to become pregnant by the Holy Spirit and would give birth to the Son of God. I was quite surprised by this but he told me everything would be okay, then he disappeared. At first I was really pleased to be pregnant with the Son of God, but then I realised that other people might not believe me, and they'd think that I wasn't a virgin – which I am. I decided to keep it quiet for the time being – just to be on the safe side – but I knew that I'd have to tell my fiancé; otherwise he might get a bit suspicious.

Last night, he took me out for dinner so we could discuss the wedding arrangements, and I thought it would be the perfect time to tell him. Everything was going fine until the pudding. I knew I had to tell him then or I'd never do it, so I waited until he'd finished his last profiterole and then I just sort of blurted it out. He froze for a second and his eyes glazed over. I tried to explain about the angel and that I was still a virgin, but he didn't seem to believe me. He just got up and walked out, leaving me to pay the bill. I tried going round this morning but he wouldn't see me. Please help me, Aunt Belinda. I'm afraid he might cancel the wedding and I don't know what to do.

Pregnant of Nazareth

Aunt Belinda writes...

Dear Pregnant,

I don't want to worry you unnecessarily, but I don't really think that a cancelled wedding is your main concern. What you should be concerned about are the big, hard rocks the good people of Nazareth will be throwing at you, the minute word gets out that you're pregnant. I have dealt with many girls in your situation who have tried to cover their tracks by concocting some story or other to explain why they're getting bigger and bigger; I have to say, though, I've never known anyone claim they were impregnated by God himself. Ten out of ten for imagination, dear, but I'm afraid you get a big zero for plausibility. All I can suggest is that you find yourself a sprightly donkey and get as far away from Nazareth as possible. Find yourself a little village – Hebron, perhaps, or maybe Bethlehem – and lay low. The other alternative, of course, is to get that angel friend of yours to visit your fiancé and straighten everything out with him. I'm joking, of course. Good luck, girl – you're going to need it.

Mum
Wedding off stop Mary pregnant stop Not mine stop Why me stop
Joseph

Joseph
Cannot believe it stop Seemed such a nice girl stop Will you be stoning her stop
Mum

Mum
Have decided to dump her quietly stop Stoning a bit messy stop Still love her stop
Joseph

Joseph
Plenty more fish in the sea stop What about Deborah from baker's stop You'll never be short of bagels stop
Mum

Mum
Change of plans stop Wedding back on stop Angel told me God is father stop See you at the synagogue stop
Joseph

The
HEAVENLY
HOST

MEMO

To: The Heavenly Choir
From: Raphael

As part of the Almighty's new redemption initiative - dealing with sin and the causes of sin - the management requires all seraphim to report to the gates of heaven at 0300 hours. Please make sure that you have your song sheets and a clean halo with you - this is our most important booking to date and we want to look and sound our best – singers, sing with gusto; harpists, harp from the heart and trumpeters, trump like you've never trumped before! I'm counting on you, team – don't let me down.

The
HEAVENLY
HOST

Bethlehem Carol Service
Running Order

Introduction
*(Strange ethereal noises, unusual gusts of wind, **Note:** the sheep may become agitated at this point – this is perfectly normal and will probably add to the general feeling of anticipation)*

Overture
(Trumpets play a long blast – starting almost imperceptibly but building to a scarcely bearable volume. Harpists begin to play, intertwining melody and harmony in a breath-takingly beautiful tapestry of sound)

Gabriel's Entrance
(Bright flash of light, cymbal crash, short blast of 'Hallelujah!' from offstage)

Gabriel's Speech
(The shepherds will more than likely be a little overwhelmed by now, so it would probably be wise to open with a little reassuring word – 'Be not afraid!' or 'Tremble not!' or even 'Stop blubbing and listen up!' – whatever seems appropriate at the time)

Choir of Heavenly Angels
(This is the big showstopper, so we have to get it right. Myriad angels enter stage left and right and a third myriad from behind. Then it's formation flying into position and sing, sing, sing!)

Heavenly Medley
(We're very thankful to Jabeth, our musical director for this. All the old favourites are included: 'Holy, Holy, Holy', 'You are Worthy', 'My Old Man's Omnipotent', 'Maybe It's Because I'm Immortal' etc.)

Exit Choir

(On my mark, everyone disappears in the twinkling of an eye, leaving the shepherds wanting more – always leave them wanting more)

Encore

(Once the choir has disappeared, one of four things will probably happen:

1. *The shepherds will simultaneously die of fright, rendering our mission a complete failure;*
2. *The shepherds will go back to their sheep, believing the whole encounter to be a result of the curry they had earlier in the evening, in which case we have to do the whole presentation again;*
3. *The shepherds will be so excited by the news that they will run off immediately to find the baby – our mission will be a success and we can go back to base for a knees-up;*
4. *The shepherds will be so impressed by our professionalism that they shout for more, leaving us with no option but to reappear and do the encore we've been rehearsing for weeks.)*

This is a big night for us all – make me proud.

Raphael

Matthew 2:9-11

The adoration of the shepherds

New Decree Makes No Census!

Just when you thought the Romans had done all they possibly could to annoy you, they go and order a census of every man, woman and child in the country!

So can we pop down to our local centurion and hand in our details to him? Don't be silly - that's far too easy! No, the Romans decided it would be far better if everyone returned to their hometown to hand in their details; that way, thousands of people get to close up their businesses and trek for miles before handing in their details to a different centurion.

Once again, the Romans have managed to turn a stupid idea into a really stupid bureaucratic nightmare - and now towns and villages across the land are counting the cost.

Overcrowded inns, water shortages and synagogues stretched to their limit are

just some of the inevitable consequences that town officials have been struggling with over the last fortnight.

The Romans have assured us that everything will be back to normal within the month, but until then, it seems we must put up with yet more imperial red tape.

Shepherds Warning

Police are on the lookout for a band of shepherds who were creating a disturbance in Bethlehem last night. The hired hands were seen dancing through the streets singing at the top of their voices, 'Glory to God in the highest and peace to his people on earth'.

Complaints had already been made earlier about bright lights and singing coming from the field where they lay, watching their flocks by night.

Police have warned not to approach the men, as they may be religious.

Melchior – Interview with a Wise Man

Seated in a 5-star hotel room, surrounded by a small army of press officers, photographers and bodyguards, I would be forgiven for thinking that I was in the presence of royalty. I am, in fact, waiting to interview one of three celebrities made famous by a brief encounter with a baby boy.

Eventually, amid much unnecessary activity, Melchior the Wise Man appears, only seven minutes late. He is younger than I had imagined. For reasons known only to themselves, some faceless focus group decided that the public wanted *old* wise men with long, flowing beards, so the appearance of an understatedly handsome forty-something - bearded, yes, though neither long nor flowing – comes as something of a surprise. After a polite introduction, I enquire whether this tiresome, if enthusiastic, entourage is entirely necessary. He assures me, they are not his idea.

"If I had my way, it'd just be me and the lads, down at the tavern. Unfortunately, that's no longer an option. Apparently, I'm too valuable a commodity now to be let loose on my own." I find Melchior's apparent contempt for the trappings of success endearing, and so I steer the conversation towards simpler times, before the fame – as much for his sake as for mine. I wonder what it must have been like to grow up as a wise boy.

"People assume that I was always wise, but it's not true. When I was a kid I was really quite stupid. I was always getting into trouble with the teachers at school - my mum and dad despaired of me. When I left school, I was voted 'Boy Most Likely To Do Absolutely Nothing With His Life' by the staff."

This is not the answer I am expecting and Melchior smiles at my obvious surprise. "Very few wise men are naturals," he explains. "Most have fallen into wisdom purely by chance or as a last resort." I enquire which category he fell into. "Both, I suppose. After school I just kind of drifted around, falling in and out of jobs with quite spectacular regularity. I did all sorts - window cleaning, washing dishes, camel scrubbing - I was very good at cleaning things, but I just couldn't seem to hold anything down for more than a couple of weeks at a time.

"After a couple of years of this, I was feeling really low. I just felt like something was missing from my life but I didn't know what. I desperately needed something that was mine that I could take pride in. It was around this time that I was flicking through the local paper, looking for yet another job, and suddenly, there it was."

He pauses to take a sip of water from the glass next to him and I am forced to ask the question: What?

He carefully sets down his glass and continues. "A small advert at the bottom of the page. It read, 'Tired of cleaning things? Feel there's something missing from your life but you don't know what? Why not become a Wise Man and do something you can take pride in?' There was something about this ad that jumped out at me. It seemed like it had been written with me in mind. As I sat and stared at the paper, I realised that this was something I had to do. The next day, I called in at the local tech and enrolled myself on Wise Man evening classes."

Considering what Melchior has told me about his school days, I wonder why he thought Tech would be any less of a disappointment. "This was different - I can't really explain it. I just felt that this was where I was supposed to be - like it was my destiny or something."

Whatever it was - destiny or desperation - Melchior excelled at Wise Man classes and in just 3 years, graduated with honours. "The day of my graduation was one of the best of my life. My mum and dad were there, chuffed to bits, and I had finally done something worthwhile. I was a Wise Man and I had the certificate to prove it. After that, the world was my oyster."

After graduating, Wise Men can choose from a variety of careers. Most tend to move into the merchant trade or become travellers, explorers or inventors. None of these paths appealed to Melchior, however. "Me and a couple of my wise mates [Caspar and Balthazar - the other two-thirds of the famous trio] had all done well in fortune telling class, so we decided to set up a small company called *Wisdom Inc.,* advising businesses, royalty, politicians and the like on important decisions. We even had a regular astrology column in *The Daily Desert*, called *Words From The Wise*."

Not surprisingly, *Wisdom Inc.* was an instant success, with bookings all over the ancient world. The Three Wise Men, as they had become known, were the toast of both courts and companies throughout the East. As fascinating as Melchior's success story is, however, it is not his work as a fortune teller (or futurologist, as he prefers to call himself) that I want to explore, but a chance astronomical sighting, which was to change the three men's lives forever.

"One evening, Caspar and I had stayed late at the office, when Balthazar suddenly burst in and yelled at us to come and look at something outside, then he dashed out again. We dutifully followed and found Bal jumping up and down in the street pointing up at the sky - he's always been a bit of a drama queen. We looked up and there it was: the star." The star that Melchior is referring to is, of course, the now famous Bethlehem Star, which had mysteriously appeared in the Western skies. "We had no idea what it meant, but Wise Men are trained to recognise important things and there was no doubt in our minds that this was pretty big. Bal persuaded us to close the business for a few weeks and follow the star. We didn't really want to shut up shop, but being a Wise Man comes with certain responsibilities and we knew it was up to us to investigate."

And so they set off on their long journey across the desert. A journey that, considering the gravity of the occasion, was, I suggest, strangely uneventful. "It's a desert," points out Melchior, helpfully. "What did you expect, the parting of the Red Sea?" Good point.

"Once we arrived in Bethlehem, we wasted a lot of time looking in all the wrong places. Hotels, mansion houses, villas - it's amazing how dim three Wise Men can be - but nobody knew anything about a newborn king. The census made it almost impossible to get information, but we eventually found the house. I don't mind telling you, it wasn't what we expected. For a start it was in the really grimy end of Bethlehem, and the size…we didn't believe it at first, but we all felt something was drawing us towards that house.

"Balthazar was the first to the door. He stuck his head round and asked if we could come in. They told us of course we could and in we went. As we'd decked ourselves up in our best gear for the occasion, we probably would have made a real impression of wisdom and majesty, if I hadn't tripped over the doorframe and ended up in Joseph's lap. It wasn't quite the entrance we'd planned, but he and Mary were very understanding. Mary soon explained who they were and what had happened with the angel and everything and then she let me hold the baby."

So what was Jesus like, I wonder. "Everyone asks us that and I'd like to be able to say he glowed with a heavenly radiance and had a shining halo round his head, but the truth is, he was just like any other baby. There was still something amazing about it, though. Here I was, sitting in a cramped little house, cradling the Creator of the Universe in my arms. Suddenly everything seemed to come into focus and fade away at the same time. My certificate, the wisdom, the business – even my favourite camel, Gary – all seemed fantastically unimportant, as the Son of God lay there, being sick on my shoulder.

"We kipped on the floor that night and prepared to leave the next morning. Mary gave us some sandwiches for the journey and we gave her some souvenirs from our hometown, then we left for home and as far we were concerned, that was the end of it. So we weren't prepared at all for what was waiting for us back at the office."

Whilst the Wise Men had been away, word had somehow got back to their hometown of where they had been for the last month or so. "I don't know how it happened, but the first thing we saw when we turned the corner was a great multitude of people. As soon as they saw us, they set upon us like a pack of wolves. Everyone wanted to know what the house looked like, what sort of décor it had, what was Mary wearing, was the King a boy or a girl, what aftershave we wore - it was ridiculous! We were swamped with offers to appear on Christmas cards and Advent calendars and someone even wrote a song about us. All because we followed a star."

Which brings us right up to date. The trio's success shows no signs of diminishing, which means he'll be surrounded by his newfound friends for a long time to come - a fact that fills Melchior with obvious delight. "If I could dump this lot today, I would. It's a bit of a nightmare being followed around wherever you go; the trouble is, all this publicity is really good for *Wisdom Inc.* and these people are all part of the package. The lads and I have decided to go along with it for a while, for the sake of the business, but as soon as it gets too much, we're moving on." This sounds, not surprisingly, like a wise decision.

The Eastern Film Board is proud to present

They followed
a star...

...what they found
was their destiny.

RETURN OF THE MAGI

Starring

Bartimeus Yossel	Zebediah Silverstein	Jabal Shenkman
as	as	as
Melchior	Balthazar	Caspar

At a theatre near you now!

Greater Jerusalem Council
Birth Certificate

Please fill in the details of your child carefully. If any spaces are left blank, the form will be deemed incomplete and will be returned. If 'Name of Father' is left blank, the form will be returned and the mother promptly stoned. Thank you.

Name of child: *Jesus*

Date of birth: *25/12/01*

Place of birth: *In a stable, next to the Flying Camel Inn. King Street, Bethlehem*

Name of mother: *Mary*

Name of father: *Tricky one, that. Technically, we'd have to say the Lord God Almighty but, for practical, non-stoning purposes, we'll say Joseph Ben Heli.*

Signatures

Mother: .... **Father:** .... **Registrar:** ....

Nazareth Primary School
Report Card

Name Jesus Ben Joseph **Class** 4 **Teacher** Mrs Solomon

Literacy	Jesus has worked well in Literacy this year. He has a firm grasp of Aramaic, Hebrew and Greek and particularly excels in reading and understanding the scriptures.
Numeracy	Although Jesus seems to have a fairly good grasp of arithmetic, he sometimes displays an uncharacteristic disregard for the basic principles. When practising division, for example, he was adamant that he could share two fish between the whole class and still have a basket load to spare.
Science	Jesus seems to have an instinctive knowledge of how the world works and contributes well to class discussions. He does, however, need to accept when he is wrong. Only last week, he insisted that the world was round - despite all the evidence to the contrary.
Religious Education	Jesus has demonstrated a solid understanding of all the key areas of the Jewish religion. However, he can sometimes be a little over-zealous. Our class trip to the local synagogue ended in disaster after Jesus ran through the souvenir shop, overturning the tables. The school has since been banned from any future visits.
Art	Jesus has produced some beautiful pieces of art this year. He has a mastery of his materials unusual in such a young boy. He gets very excited when creating his artwork and that enthusiasm is infectious - the other children seem to become more creative when Jesus is around.

DT	*Not surprisingly, being the son of a carpenter, Jesus has shown great promise in DT. He is able to produce the most beautiful objects out of seemingly nothing. I have no idea how he does it!*
Personal & Social	*Jesus has, once again, had no trouble making friends this year. Children just seem to want to be around him - as do the teachers for that matter! He just needs to realise that he cannot always be right. Nobody's perfect - not even Jesus!*
General	*I have never taught a child like Jesus before. He has been a delight to have in the class and I shall miss him very much when he leaves. Well done, Jesus. Keep it up!*

Have you seen this boy?

Police are looking for a 12 year-old boy named Jesus Ben Joseph. He has been missing for two days now, since he was separated from his mother and father whilst leaving Jerusalem for Nazareth. If you have seen Jesus, or know of his whereabouts, please give him a good thrashing on behalf of his parents who are worried sick and then contact the Jerusalem Constabulary on 735129.

The boy's parents describe Jesus as medium height, with no distinguishing marks. They also describe him as very intelligent and well mannered, although we at the Jerusalem Constabulary would question just how intelligent and well mannered it is to leave the safety of his parents' side and go gallivanting off in a busy city such as this.

It's not as if we don't have anything better to do with our time than to search the back streets of Jerusalem during the busiest week of the year, looking for disobedient young tearaways who think the world revolves around them. If it were up to us, we'd lock them all up and throw away the key. Nevertheless, the boy's parents *would* like to find him as soon as possible so that they can be on their way home.

Thank you.

To: Joseph Ben Heli
        Joseph's Wood Shop
        Nazareth
        Galilee

Dear Mr. Ben Heli,

I am writing to you concerning your son, Jesus. As I am sure you will remember, some of my colleagues and I met your son last month in the temple courts in Jerusalem. Although this was, I am sure, a very distressing time for you and your wife – not knowing where your son was and all – it was also, I believe, a significant meeting for us in the Sanhedrin.

As I am sure you are aware, Mr. Ben Heli, we live in troubled times. Our beloved land is under occupation and it is all that we Pharisees can do to keep the purity of the nation's spiritual life alive. Which brings me to Jesus. It was obvious to us all last month that your son is uncommonly blessed with a depth of knowledge of the scriptures surpassing that of some of our less senior members. He was able to hold his own in a number of situations, such as *Scripture Twenty Questions*, *Scripture Trivia*, *What's My Theology?* and he even beat Donald three times in a row at Chess. These are not the actions of an ordinary child, Mr Ben Heli.

I am writing, then, to encourage you and your wife to consider Jesus for membership of the Sanhedrin. Obviously, being only twelve years old, he is too young at the moment – whoever heard of a twelve year-old Pharisee? - but once he turns thirteen, he will be a man and we would be very happy to have him in our number. Of course, that would mean that you would have to cut all ties with him, but I'm sure you have other children to keep you busy. I do not believe that last month's meeting was by chance, Mr. Ben Heli. This is your son's destiny – to stand shoulder to shoulder with his fellow Pharisees against imperfection, impurity and ignorance.

You will find enclosed an application form for Jesus to fill in once he has celebrated his bar mitzvah. Just send it back to me and we can have a camel sent round to Nazareth in no time. Think about it, Mr. Ben Heli. I look forward to hearing from you.

Yours

Jonah Ben Eliakim
Staffing, The Sanhedrin

The Sanhedrin
Helping you to do it our way

Application Form

Please answer the questions in the spaces provided. Do not write beyond the lines provided. Do not use any colour ink other than black. Do not use joined-up writing. Do not ramble on any more than you have to. Do not doodle in the margins. Do not use incorrect punctuation.
Thank you for considering the Sanhedrin.

Name: ....

Address: ....

....

....

Age: ....

Occupation: ....

Why do you want to join the Sanhedrin?

....

....

....

What talents or gifts would you bring to the Sanhedrin?

....

....

....

What makes you think you're holy enough to be in the Sanhedrin?

....

....

....

Pharisees have a reputation for being arrogant, pig-headed, rude, unsociable, conceited, proud and egotistical. What would you do to maintain that reputation?

....

....

....

How much money do you have?

....

Are you prepared to wear a phylactery on your head at all times?

....

Do you look good in a dress?

....

Are you willing to give a tenth of your herbs and spices to the temple?

....

Give three reasons why you are holier than your neighbour:

....

....

The Department of Health and Safety - Food Division

To: John the Baptist
The River Jordan
Salim
Galilee

Dear Mr. the Baptist,

I am writing to you to express my reservations concerning your somewhat unorthodox lifestyle. The Department of Health and Safety – Food Division (DHS-FD) exists to monitor and improve the dietary habits of the general public and I am afraid that your 'prophetic' lifestyle has given us cause for concern.

The DHS-FD has gone to a great deal of trouble to encourage the general public to adopt a healthy, balanced diet, helping to ensure good health, long life and a general feeling of well being. With this in mind, I regret to inform you, Mr. the Baptist, that locusts and wild honey is not such a diet. Now, I am sure the honey provides plenty of much-needed energy – vital when wandering about the wilderness – and I have no doubt that the locusts contain some proteins and vitamins useful for maintaining good health, but you cannot, by any stretch of the imagination, call this a balanced diet. Where are the vegetables? Where is the vitamin C? And where is the calcium? I shudder to think what condition your teeth must be in after all that honey.

You have to understand that you are a high-profile individual and, as such, you have considerable influence over the lifestyle choices of those who look up to you, and I am afraid that this diet of yours is undermining a great deal of good work that we are doing in schools across the country. With fame comes responsibility, Mr. the Baptist, and I am urging you to face up to that responsibility by encouraging your admirers to eat a healthy, balanced diet. With this in mind, I would like you to consider endorsing our new Healthy Eating campaign. I have enclosed a sample poster for you to look at and I would be interested to hear your thoughts. I look forward to hearing from you and, hopefully, working with you.

Yours in anticipation,

Joel Ben Achmed
Director, Department of Health and Safety – Food Division

You can't beat a good locust!

Especially
when it's
served with
carrots,
peas
and
mashed
potatoes!

Even the most unusual foods taste better with a healthy selection of
vegetables and a cool glass of milk to wash it down.
So what are you waiting for?
Take the plunge with John the Baptist and eat the healthy way today!

For reasons that escaped John, his friends never seemed to be available for subsequent dinner parties

Baps - Cont.

Barry's Baps
For that great taste of traditional homemade baps, look no further than Barry's Baps. Baps to suit every occasion!
Ring: 864325

Baptists

Bob the Baptist
Feeling guilty?
Can't look the rabbi in the eye?

Sounds like you need to be baptised!
Most sins guaranteed to be washed away.
(*Will consider more extreme sins at an extra cost*)
Ring 764528 for a free written quotation!

Confused about who to be baptised with?
Well, why not go with

Joel the Baptist
Laban brings expertise, elegance and entertainment to your baptism experience.
You only get baptised once – so get baptised by the best!
Call 646321 for an instant quotation.
A member of The Baptisers' Guild

John The Baptist
If you are serious about turning back to God, then come and be baptised.
No time wasters.

Michael the Baptist

Kids' parties a speciality. Bring yours along for a baptism to remember!
Each child gets a free baptismal goodie bag!

Ring 123865 for details.

Baptism Accessories

Jabesh's Baptismal Superstore

For all your baptismal needs!
Competitive prices and excellent service.
1 mile south of the Sea of Galilee, on the east bank of the Jordan.
Ring 649785.

For a great family day out and the chance to say 'Goodbye' to your sins, you can't beat
Baptisms 'R' Us
We are three miles east of Jericho – just follow the signs!
Call us on 665332

The Baptism Warehouse
The one-stop shop for baptismal gowns, waterproof sandals, snorkels and quick sketch artists (to record the happy occasion)!
Baptisms are our business!
Ring 645821

Barbarians

Simon the Barbarian

Are your neighbours annoying you?
Are you getting bullied at school?
Does your boss need bringing down a peg or two?

Why not hire **Simon the Barbarian** to sort them out?

He's not subtle but he'll get the job done!

Ring 642315 for details.

Barbers

Desert Delights

For the more discerning customer. If you want to turn heads at parties, we can give you a style to dye for!
Ring Colin on 462315

Bards

Lamesh's Entertainments
Entertainers to royalty
Music, song and dancers provided for all types and sizes of party.
Reasonable rates.
Dance of the Seven Veils our speciality.
Can be as tasteful or sleazy as you like.
Ring Lamesh on 865321.

World Leaders' Digest
Prize Notification!

Jesus Ben Joseph - you may already have won this lovely hot and crusty loaf of bread!

Dear Jesus,

Your name has been chosen out of the millions of names in the Jewish nation to qualify for a chance to own your own loaf of warm, crusty bread! **Yes, it's true, Jesus!** I know how hungry a man can get wandering about in the wilderness for <u>forty days and forty nights</u> with absolutely **nothing** to eat or drink. That's why we at World Leaders' Digest <u>know</u> that you will not be able to resist this **fabulous prize**!

The loaf of bread that you could win is <u>extra large, extra crusty and extra delicious!</u> I'll even throw in a pot of jam **out of my own kitchen cupboard!**

So what is it that you have to do to win this loaf? **It's simple!** On the reverse of this letter you will find attached a small rock. All you have to do is use your powers as the <u>Son of God</u> to turn this rock into that mouth-watering loaf of bread! **It's as easy as that!**

And, as if the loaf of bread wasn't enough, we're going to give you the opportunity to prove your Messiahship to the whole world in <u>one easy step!</u> Just put a tick in the box below and we will arrange for you to be taken to the very top of the temple in Jerusalem. From there, you will be in **prime position** to reveal your unique relationship with God! All you have to do is step off the temple and plummet to a certain and bloody death below, knowing, of course, that you will be caught by a **crack team** of angels before you even strike your foot against a stone. This act will prove, beyond a shadow of a doubt, your superiority over mankind!

And just in case you were thinking it couldn't get any better than that – **think again** - because we have one final prize that outshines even the tastiest loaf of bread – <u>lordship over all the kingdoms of the earth!</u> Yes, that's right, Jesus, every kingdom and its king will bow down to you forever – and all you have to do is this one, <u>ridiculously simple</u> act: bow down and worship my **good friend**, Satan. Yes, Jesus, you read correctly! You bow down to one, single person and, in return, every other person on earth will bow down to you. It's madness, I know, but it's yours for the taking, Jesus. **This is your lucky day!**

You're probably thinking that this is all too good to be true! 'I won't win - nobody ever wins these things'. Well, here are a few <u>actual quotes</u> from previous competition winners:

"When I was offered riches, splendour <u>and</u> success in battle, I thought it must have been some kind of elaborate joke, but you delivered everything you promised! Thanks, World Leaders' Digest!"

Nebuchadnezzar, King of Babylon

"It's amazing! One minute I was a humble office clerk, then I received my prize notification letter from World Leaders' Digest and before I knew it, I was the most powerful man of my generation!"

Rameses I, Egyptian Pharaoh

"I can't thank the people of World Leaders' Digest enough! You turned my little republic into a fantastic empire! Thanks again!"

Julius Caesar, Roman Emperor

And these are just a few of the hundreds of prize winners whose lives have been changed by World Leaders' Digest - so you see, Jesus, you don't just have to take my word for it!

All that's left for you to do now is tick the boxes in the form below and return it to me in order to activate your **fabulous** prizes! And if you tick all three, we'll send you a beautifully crafted **gold effect** pen <u>free of charge</u>!

Yours in excited anticipation,

Tobias Champagne
World Leaders' Digest

- -

I, Jesus, am very excited to hear about my prizes and I can't believe that all I have to do is:

☐ Use my Son-of-God powers to turn the attached rock into a delicious loaf of bread.

☐ Jump off the temple roof and let angels catch me, thus proving my power to all the world

☐ Bow down and worship Satan in order to rule the kingdoms of the world.

Please hurry my prizes to me as soon as possible.

Jesus Ben Joseph

W'ords from the W'ise

Friday, August 2nd

Aries - Mar 21 – Apr 19

The time couldn't be better for you to sell your family and begin a new life as a travelling minstrel. Go on – take the plunge!

Lucky elephant: African

Taurus - Apr 20 – May 20

Venus is in the depths of depression this week – which is good news for you! Why not go out and buy yourself a new sheep to celebrate?

Lucky nut: Almond

Gemini - May 21 – Jun 21

A chance meeting with a fishmonger on Monday will lead inexorably to a life of adventure on the ocean wave. Don't forget your scarf.

Unlucky tree: Sycamore

Cancer - Jun 22 – Jul 22

What worked wonderfully well for you last week will end in almost certain tragedy this week; so don't try it – not even a bit.

Lucky mammal: Mole

Leo - July 23 – Aug 22

Saturn's orbit has gone all wobbly this week, so it's probably best to keep away from dairy products – just to be on the safe side.

Unlucky continent: Australasia

Virgo - Augt 23 – Sep 22

On Wednesday morning, you will receive an invitation out of the blue to a high school reunion. Stay away - it's a trap!

Lucky meal: Lamb Hot Pot

Libra - Sep 23 – Oct 22

Romance is just around the corner for Librans this week. Whatever you do, don't wear your blue hat or it could all blow up in your face.

Unlucky hairstyle: Beehive

Scorpio - Oct 23 – Nov 21

Camel farming will be high up on the agenda this week, but you need to decide if it really is what you want to do with your life.

Lucky dessert: Profiteroles

Sagittarius - Nov 22 – Dec 21

The words 'elbow' and 'underlay' will almost certainly loom large in your astrological bearings this week. Use them wisely.

Lucky steak: Tenderloin

Capricorn - Dec 22 – Jan 19

You're feeling a bit under the weather this week - like the fate of the whole world is resting on your shoulders. Well, maybe it is.

Unlucky expression: Confused

Aquarius - Jan 20 – Feb 18

You're wondering whether or not to buy that shiny new cart down at the market place. Wonder no longer – it's already been sold.

Lucky river: The Euphrates

Pisces - Feb 19 – Mar 20

Due to planetary alignments, Monday will officially be the best day of your life. Be sure to set the alarm – it's all down hill from Tuesday.

Lucky biscuit: Custard Cream

Matthew 8:14-15

Peter was overjoyed to see that Jesus
had healed his mother-in-law

The Temple of God
JERUSALEM
"always a sacrifice-never a chore"

Subject: Daniel Ben Simeon

Case: Cessation of demon possession

Witness: Colin Ben Tracy

Occupation of Witness: Chief Hair Stylist, Desert Delights

In order for the priest in charge to better ascertain the subject's condition, it is necessary for the witness to provide a written account of the events surrounding his alleged cleansing. Please try to be brief and to the point.

Well, it all happened last Thursday about 11:15 in the morning. I know it was that time because Nigel always makes a nice cup of tea for us at eleven on the dot, bless him. Nigel's our assistant at the salon, by the way. He hasn't been with us very long, but he's showing great promise. He's very good with the customers – which is important – and he does make a lovely cup of tea. Hits the spot every time. Anyway, I distinctly remember my cup was still half full when the gentleman in question showed up, because Mrs. Cohen knocked it a little with the fright and spilt a drop on my copy of Style Monthly. Not to worry – these things happen. There wasn't much in this month's anyway, which is unusual because it's normally got some interesting articles.

Anyway, you're probably not interested in that, so I'll get straight to the point. I was just adding the finishing touches to Mrs. Cohen's Paradise Perm when, out of nowhere, in walks your man, bold as you like, naked as the day he was born. Now, you can imagine that this is not the sort of thing that you would normally come across at the Gergesa branch. Mr. Bloomsdale must have been spinning in his tomb. He's our founder. He died a few years ago but not before building up a successful chain of *Desert Delights* salons stretching from Tyre all the way down to Jericho. He was an inspiration to us all, but he was very concerned about setting standards and I don't think a naked man with hair down to his ankles was quite the image he was after.

Nevertheless, there he was, just standing and staring. We all knew who he was, of course. Hairy naked people are reasonably rare in these parts - especially at this time of year – and we'd all heard the stories about Demon Dan, the crazy man. He used to live amongst the tombs on the north side of town, just running around, howling and scaring the tourists. I wouldn't go to that side of town myself, you understand. You never know who you're going to run in to.

It's fair to say, then, that we were all somewhat taken aback by his appearance. As I mentioned before, Mrs. Cohen jumped out of her skin and spilt my tea, but that wasn't the worst of it. I don't have to tell you that a decent Paradise Perm is a precision work of art – one that requires complete stillness and concentration - so when poor Mrs. Cohen jumped in her seat, my implements were scattered everywhere, throwing the whole creation into disarray. It wasn't pretty, I can tell you, but there was nothing I could do about it. I don't know what upset me most – the sight of this brute at my door or the sight of one of my creations ruined.

Now I admit that I'm not what you would call the heroic type and normally I would have run as fast as I could in the opposite direction, but something inside me just snapped. So with all my strength, I shouted to Nigel to do something. Unfortunately, Nigel was crouching behind the blow dryers, sobbing - poor boy. I knew then that it was up to me to stop him. I looked around for something to defend myself with – I couldn't use my scissors, they were too precious. The only things that were handy were the rollers I was using on Mrs. Cohen, so I pulled out a handful from the shoulder bag my mother made for me and threw them at Demon Dan. Incredibly, they just bounced off his big hairy chest and fell to the floor.

That was it. I thought we were all done for. Demon Dan stared straight at me with eyes as wild as the night and slowly began to walk across the salon. By this time, Mrs. Cohen had abandoned her chair and was whimpering behind the sink. As he moved closer, all I could think of was how I could restore her perm to its former glory, but it was too late for that now. There I was, standing face to face with a six-foot lunatic, all naked and quivering before me. I frantically tried to remember if this situation had been covered in styling classes but alas, this was a scenario that even Mr. Bloomsdale himself could not have anticipated. I tossed my one remaining roller at him in a last, pathetic attempt to defend myself, and then I closed my eyes and prepared myself for the worst. After what seemed like an eternity, he spoke.

"Could I have a haircut, please?"

It took a second to sink in. I eventually managed to open an eye and Demon Dan's face somehow didn't seem that demonic anymore. "I'm sorry?" I managed to whisper.

"Could I have a haircut, please?"

I couldn't believe it.

"But aren't you Demon Dan the crazy man?" I asked, rather stupidly, I admit.

"I was," he replied, "but I'm just Dan now. Do you have any trousers?"

I was so taken aback by the fact that I was still alive, I had completely forgotten that he was still naked. "Of course. Nigel, give Dan your trousers, please." I was only too willing to help.

"Thank you" came the softly spoken reply. "Now about that haircut…"

And as he spoke those words, my fear left me and I was struck with an overwhelming sense of purpose. This is what my whole life had been leading up to. This was my destiny. Here was a man who hadn't even *seen* a hairdressing salon in decades – perhaps ever! A tangled, dishevelled forest of a man – and he wanted – needed – me to deliver him from his wilderness of style. All at once, inspiration flowed like a raging torrent through my consciousness. There were endless possibilities just waiting to be explored. I felt like a master painter and this was my canvas.

I ordered everyone to leave the salon, Mrs. Cohen included. This was something I had to do alone. As I began on my hairdressing odyssey, Dan told me how he had had countless demons cast out of him by a young man called Jesus. He spoke excitedly about this miracle worker throughout the afternoon, and as he talked, I was inspired to work one or two miracles of my own.

My Summer

This sumer I went to my nan and grandads for the hollidaze. They live in a small villige called bethany. I made a new frend. He was called Jared. We cort some frogs and put them in a jar but they eskaped befor we cud do experrymunts on them. I went home.

By Mark

A good effort, Mark. Maybe a bit longer next time.

My Summer

This summer I went to my Uncle Reuben's house in Jerusilum. We went to the tempul and bought a sheep to sakrifise. The preest did lots of horribul things to it but Uncle Reuben said that God was pleesed, so that's OK. Uncle Reuben let me biy a dove at the temple market to take home. I called it Dave. I am trying to teach it triks but all it does is sit on its purch and coo. If it doesn't jump throogh my ring of fire soon, I am going to take it back to Jerusilum and get the preest to sakrifise it.

By Simon

Lovely work, Simon.

My summer

This summer I staid at home because I was ill. I bilt a model of the sinagog out of machsticks but my brother nocked it down. Then I drew some pichurs of the street and the vyew from my bedroom window. I cudn't do much when I got wurse, so my mum just talked to me and told me storys. Then I got so sick that I died, but a nice man called Jesus came and made me beter. After that, I wasn't ill enimore so I cud play out with my frends.

By Rachel

Very nice, Rachel.

Home Sweet Home for Miracle Man?

Miracle Maker, Jesus of Nazareth, who has been gaining support and popularity throughout the country, seems to have hit a brick wall in his hometown! Jesus, 30, has already wowed crowds both in Galilee and Jerusalem with his amazing miraculous feats. Healing the blind, the lame, the deaf and some say even the dead, Jesus has become the toast of every town he has visited.

That is, until he went to his hometown of Nazareth two days ago. When Jesus first entered the gates on Sunday morning, he was greeted by the customary crowds, but awe soon turned to resentment, as people began to question why they should listen to 'little Jesus from three doors down', as one lady put it.

It seems nobody wants salvation from someone they went to school with, and so Jesus, not wanting to force himself on anyone, cut his meeting short and visited his mother, Mary, for some home-cooked lamb hot pot. When asked why he was leaving, Jesus commented, 'a prophet is without honour only in his own town.' He also confirmed that he had no plans to cancel subsequent dates in the surrounding area.

Personals

Birthdays

Salome   **16th Birthday**
To my darling Salome on her 16th birthday. It doesn't seem long ago since you were my cute little baby niece, and now you've grown up to be my very own beautiful daughter. Hope you like the head, Sweetie.

Love and kisses,
Herod

Deaths

Rachel   **Aug 16th**
Beloved daughter of Jairus and Jessica. We'll always love you.

Lots of love,
Mummy and Daddy

John (the Baptist)   **Aug 13th**
He was an inspiration to thousands and a friend to his disciples. He brought many back to God, spoke out against injustice and foretold the coming of the Messiah – and all this brought to an end by a spoilt little teenager. You will be sadly missed, but your message lives on.

The Baptists

Resurrections

Rachel   **Aug 16th**
Beloved daughter of Jairus and Jessica. Welcome back, Rachel! Thanks be to God!
Lots of love,
Mummy and Daddy

Classified

AAA Brass Bell For Sale
Previously owned by leper. Very good condition, on account of nobody ever coming anywhere near it. Sale due to miraculous recovery. Bell has subsequently been cleansed and blessed by a priest, along with owner.

Accomodation

House For Sale
Good condition except for big hole in roof. Makes a good conversation starter and creates a pleasing through draught in the summer.
Viewings are encouraged *after* contracts have been exchanged. For further information and a free copy of *'101 Things To Do With A Hole In Your Roof'*, ring 643215.

To: King Herod Antipas
         The Palace
         Jerusalem
         Judea

Dear Mr. Antipas,

I am writing to you concerning the party you held at your palace last week in honour of your daughter Salome's 16th birthday. It is my understanding that you had a substantial finger buffet, which included boiled elephant trunk, sliced and served with sour cream and chive dip, peacock beak vol au vents and gazelle heart canapés. This was, I am sure, delicious, but I am afraid that if my reports are correct, there was a serious breach of health and safety regulations during the fish course.

According to my report, your delightful daughter danced the Dance of the Seven Veils at your request and for your guests' pleasure. I believe that this was truly a sight to behold – unfortunately, it led directly to the regulation breach in question. As I understand it, you were heard to promise anything up to half your kingdom to Salome in return for her performance. A generous offer, I must say, but it backfired somewhat when your sweet young daughter requested the head of John the Baptist on a platter.

Now, far be it from me to be giving tips on raising teenagers to the king of Israel, but I do believe that granting this request was a mistake – not because of any moral or religious objection but because the freshly severed head of a man whose personal hygiene was, at best, unusual, is frankly a bit of a no-no as far as fresh food and party catering is concerned. I very much doubt that the head had been cleaned up or sterilised before being brought to the party and, though I don't possess an in-depth knowledge of the human anatomy, I am guessing that a wound such as the Baptist's would produce a not inconsiderable amount of blood. Now, I know that the head was produced on a silver platter, as requested, but unless the platter was a good 15 inches deep, I would imagine that some blood was spilt on the floor.

As I mentioned above, this action does amount to a breaching of our health and safety regulations and this would normally result in the closing down of the establishment at fault. However, as the establishment at fault is the royal palace and you are the king of Israel, capable of serving up *my* head on a silver platter, I am willing to look the other way on this occasion. Though I would ask that, should you, in the future, decide to serve up any further dismembered body parts to your dinner guests, you would do it over brandy and cigars when the food has been safely tidied away.

Thank you for your time.

Yours sincerely,

Joel Ben Achmed
Director, Department of Health and Safety – Food Division

Salome felt sure her contribution to Show and Tell would beat Freddy's dead frog hands down

Disciples' Evangelism Exercise
ASSESSMENT SHEET

Names: Simon Peter
Andrew

Region Covered: The Decapolis

Number of villages visited: 9

Number of villages blessed: 6

Number of villages whose dust was shaken from feet: 3

If dust was shaken from feet, please state reasons:

Two villages did not accept our teaching. The people of the third village said that Peter had a big nose.

Number of people healed: 37

Number of healing attempts: 54

If number is different, please state reasons:

Lack of faith on their part. Plus it was very hot, which made it hard to concentrate - and we were just warming up on the first few goes. It looked much easier when Jesus did it.

Give details of any other miracles performed whilst preaching the word:

Peter actually refused a fourth helping of chicken casserole in Caesarea. Oh, and Andrew raised a dead woman in Pella.

Number of people saved: 46

What insights have you gained?

Never try to save a person's soul immediately after eating garlic for lunch.

- -

(For office use only)

General Comments:

The boys have had a successful few days. Peter needs to be a bit less sensitive about his nose, but otherwise, a good start to what promises to be a great ministry.

Signed: Jesus (Christ)

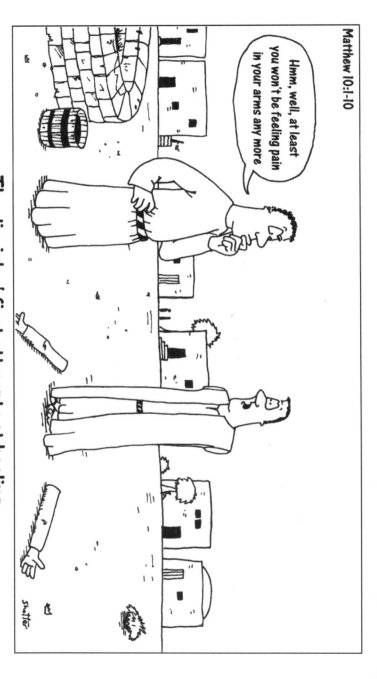

The disciples' first attempts at healing didn't always go according to plan

Disciples' Evangelism Exercise
ASSESSMENT SHEET

Names: James
John

Region Covered: Galilee (West)

Number of villages visited: 8

Number of villages blessed: 6

Number of villages whose dust was shaken from feet: 2

If dust was shaken from feet, please state reasons:

The villagers wouldn't accept our teaching. We tried calling down hailstones but they didn't come.

Number of people healed: 28

Number of healing attempts: 37

If number is different, please state reasons:

They did not believe that God would heal them. In the end, we decided to call down plagues and pestilence on the unbelievers. Nothing happened, though.

Give details of any other miracles performed whilst preaching the word:

We called down fiery rain on one unbeliever's house and it started to rain. They were actually quite pleased as it hadn't rained for ages.

Number of people saved: 37

What insights did you gain?

There are so many unbelievers out there, it's difficult to know what curse to call down on who.

(For office use only)

General Comments:

Another successful outing - despite feeling the need to call down punishment on anyone who disagrees with them. They've still got a lot to learn about grace!

Signed: Jesus (Christ)

As well as Jesus' successful healing and teaching ministry, he and his disciples were also a crack crime-fighting team

Disciples' Evangelism Exercise
ASSESSMENT SHEET

Names: Judas Iscariot
Bartholomew

Region Covered: The Decapolis

Number of villages visited: 5

Number of villages blessed: 5

Number of villages whose dust was shaken from feet: 0

If dust was shaken from feet, please state reasons:

All this shaking of dust from one's feet is very uncivilised. Tolerance is surely the best way to win support.

Number of people healed: 1

Number of healing attempts: 0

If number is different, please state reasons:

We thought it best, as we were doing a lot of travelling and speaking, to keep away from sick people as much as we could. The man who was healed had a cold that eased up while we were there.

Give details of any other miracles performed whilst preaching the word:

Barth tried and failed to heal a girl with measles in the first village we visited, so I banned him from any more miracle attempts – to save embarrassment.

Number of people saved: 0

What insights have you gained?

We really need to repackage the whole 'repent and be baptised' thing. It's far too stark for the modern punter.

(For office use only)

General Comments:

I think I need to have a word with Judas.
Note to self: send Bartholomew with somebody else next time.

Signed: Jesus (Christ)

Dear Obed,

How are you, my friend? The northern air is doing you good, I hope. I realise that you weren't very keen when the Sanhedrin posted you in Galilee, but in these uncertain times we must take what is given.

Now, to business. As you know, we Pharisees are always on the lookout for the Messiah - the chosen one of God who will rise up and deliver his people from the hands of their enemies – and I want you to keep an eye out for him up in Galilee. Now, I realise that the chances of the Messiah turning up anywhere north of Ephraim are remote at best, but we must not be seen to be negligent in our duties as God's representatives on earth.

You, therefore, have two months in which to put together a list of possible candidates for the Messiahship. I want details of each one, including interviews with the candidates themselves plus any other witnesses to miracles, signs and wonders and any miscellaneous Messiah-like tendencies. I'll expect your report on my desk soon - I look forward to reading it.

That will be all, Obed. Happy hunting – and say hello to your mother for me.

Yours,

Jacob
(Pharisee-in-charge – Messianic division)

Obed Ben Rabath

Pharisee and Sanhedrin
Galilean Representative

Will preside over weddings, funerals and bar mitzvahs

Dear Jacob,

Thank you for your letter. I appreciate your concern, but I'm doing fine up here, thanks. The air is fresh and the pace is far less stressful than down there in Jerusalem.

I will, of course, do as you asked, though I have to say, I don't share your scepticism about Galilee. If the stories I'm hearing are true, I'm going to be very busy indeed. But you'll be able to read all about it in my report.

I look forward to speaking to you in person.

Yours,

Obed

P.S. Mother says 'Hi'!

Are you the Messiah?

For centuries, the people of God have been waiting for the Messiah – the Chosen One, spoken of by Moses and the prophets, who will lead our nation to victory over all our enemies and bring peace and prosperity to this Promised Land. Holy men have, for years, been looking for a sign that the time is right for that Messiah.

We, the Sanhedrin, believe that time is now.

If you believe that you could be the Messiah, we need to speak with you and, as guardians of the faith and spiritual leaders of the People of God, we know that you will want to speak to us. Just ask yourself these six simple questions to be certain of your destiny…

1. Are you zealous for the Lord, your God, and his Chosen People?
2. Do you weep to see God's Chosen People held captive by their enemies?
3. Are you willing and able to lead an army into battle against these enemies?
4. Is there any history of heart trouble in your family?
5. Would you be willing to travel?
6. Do you recognise the members of the Sanhedrin as your spiritual leaders?

If you answered 'Yes' to these questions (except Question 4), then you may be just the man we're looking for.
Contact your local Sanhedrin representative for details and remember – the future of God's Chosen People could be in your hands.

There's always one

Dear Jesus,

Thank you for visiting our school last week. You are a very nice man. I liked it best when you turned the pebbles into lollies. You can come again.

Love Nathan

Dear Jesus,

Thank you for visiting us. I think you are all right.

Love Jessica

Dear Jesus,

You are a nice man. You tell funny stories. I wish you were my uncle. Please come again.

Love Deborah

Dear Jesus,

My daddy says you are a profit, but you don't seem to have any money at all. Do you know my daddy? He is nice. I think you would like him.

Love Kirsty

Dear Jesus,

My daddy says that you are John the Baptist and my granddad says you might be Elijah. My rabbi thinks you are Jeremiah and I think you look like my Uncle William. Who do you think you are? Do you know? Thanks for the lolly.

Love Jacob

Dear Jesus,

You came to my school. You have a beard.

Love Daniel

Dear Jesus,

That trick with the pebbles and the lollies was pretty neat. Please can I have my pebble collection back now?

Love Christopher

Dear Jesus,

Thank you for healing Sparky, our pet hamster. He is much better now. Mrs. Davies thinks he might be pregnant. You are very clever.

Love Stephanie

Dear Jesus,

I know how you did that trick with the pebbles. I'm still trying to work out how you made Sparky better. Do you know any more tricks?

Love Graham

Dear Jesus,

Thank you for making our hamster better. You should try that with people. It might work.

Love Amy

Dear Jesus,

You are a very nice man. You should meet my uncle in Jerusalem. He is a Pharisee. He talks about God too. He would like you a lot, I think.

Love Jonathan

Dear Jesus,

I heard someone call you the son of David. My daddy is called David too. Maybe we are brothers.

Love Carl

Dear Jesus,

Thank you for not telling Mrs. Davies when I kicked Daniel. I tried not to do it again like you said, but I think you might kick him too if you had to sit next to him.

Love Bernard

Dear Jesus,

Thanks for the lolly. It was the nicest I've ever had and I've had a lot. Do you have a shop?

Love Sophie

Dear Jesus,

You are a nice man. Keep it up.

Love Emily

Dear Jesus,

I liked your story about the good shepherd. I'm glad that God is nice. He needs to be with me.

Love Thomas

Dear Jesus,

You seem to know a lot about God. Maybe you should be a Pharisee.

Love Susan

Dear Jesus,

Thank you for telling us about God. How come our rabbi doesn't know as many stories as you? Maybe you could write some down for him.

Love Jack

The Temple of God
JERUSALEM
"always a sacrifice-never a chore"

TRANSCRIPT OF INTERVIEW

Messiah Candidate: Jesus of Nazareth

Evidence of Messiahship: Alleged transformation of water into wine

Name of witnesses: Margaret Golding, Elizabeth Jacobs

Occupation of Witnesses: Retired

OBED: The interview begins at the seventh hour. I am Obed Ben Rabath and I am interviewing Mrs. Margaret Golding and Mrs. Elizabeth Jacobs.

JACOBS: Hello.

GOLDING: Hello.

OBED: Hello. I am interviewing them about an incident involving Jesus of Nazareth at the wedding of Jeth Ben Abel at Cana last year. Mrs. Jacobs, could you tell me what your relationship is with Jesus of Nazareth?

JACOBS: Yes, dear. Me and Marge are very good friends of his mother, Mary. We've watched little Jesus grow from a tiny little baby to the big, strapping man he is today.

GOLDING: Ooh, he is lovely, that Jesus, you know. He's so thoughtful. Mary never seems to have any trouble with him at all – not like ours, Betty.

JACOBS: Oh, I know. Where did we go wrong, Marge?

GOLDING: We had sons, Betty.

OBED: Erm, right, thank you. Now, could you tell me exactly what happened at the wedding, with particular regard to Jesus?

JACOBS: Ooh, yes, I remember it as if it were yesterday.

GOLDING: Which is amazing, considering the amount of wine she consumed.

JACOBS: Thank you, Marge. I don't think the gentleman wants to hear your silly comments.

GOLDING: I'm just saying.

JACOBS: Anyway, we were only half-way through the sixth course.

GOLDING: A lovely roast quail with tiny little roast shallots.

JACOBS: That's right, when all of a sudden, a couple of servants appear looking white as a sheet and whisper something to the head of the banquet. Well, Mary was close by and she overheard them saying that they'd run out of wine!

GOLDING: It's a disgrace, really.

JACOBS: It is. Mind you, there *were* seventeen courses in all, but still.

OBED: What happened, then? Did the guests walk out?

JACOBS: No.

OBED: Was there a fight?

GOLDING: Well, there probably would have been if Jesus hadn't been there.

OBED: Why, does he make his own wine?

GOLDING: Well, sort of.

OBED: What do you mean?

JACOBS: Well, when Mary overheard the caterers, she just leans over to her Jesus and says, "Ey up, son, they've run out of wine."

OBED: And what did Jesus do?

JACOBS: Well, he just turns to his mother and says to her, bold as brass, "Woman, why do you involve me? My time has not yet come."

GOLDING: That's no way to talk to your mother.

JACOBS: I know.

OBED: What did he mean? Wasn't his homemade stuff ready yet?

JACOBS: Well, apparently, Mary got up anyway and told the caterers to do whatever Jesus told them to do.

GOLDING: She had a bit of a cheek if you ask me.

JACOBS: Nobody did ask you, Marge.

OBED: So what did he do?

JACOBS: Well, he got up and told them to fill six great big jars full of water.

OBED: Water?

GOLDING: Plain, ordinary water.

OBED: And did they?

JACOBS: Yep. They had over 150 gallons of the stuff by the time they were finished.

GOLDING: It just seemed like a waste of time to us. They could have been down to the off-licence and back by then.

JACOBS: But it gets better. When they'd finished filling all the jars, Jesus told them to serve it to the guests.

OBED: Serve the water?

JACOBS: I'm just telling you what happened.

OBED: Was he trying to make the groom look stupid or something?

JACOBS: Will you let me finish?

OBED: Sorry.

JACOBS: The water was given to the master of the banquet to taste and everyone thought he was going to spit it out, but he didn't.

OBED: What did he do, then?

JACOBS: He takes another gulp and then he leans over to the groom and he says, "People usually bring out the best wine first and then the plonk later on, when the guests have had a few too many, but you have saved the best till last."

OBED: Incredible!

GOLDING: Then, the caterers start ladling it out to the other guests and it was all wine! All 150 gallons of it.

OBED: I don't believe it!

JACOBS: And Jesus just sits back down, calm as anything, and carries on eating his roast quail.

OBED: And do you have any idea how Jesus did this trick?

MARGE: It wasn't a trick, young man - it was a miracle from God.

OBED: Well, I think we'll leave that for the Sanhedrin to decide.

MARGE: Now, listen, young man. I know what I saw that day and it wasn't a trick and it wasn't a wine-making kit.

OBED: Thank you, ladies. The interview is over.

JACOBS: I don't know, he puts on a dress and a silly hat and he thinks he knows everything.

OBED: It is not a dress it is a ceremonial gown. Thank you, that will be all, ladies. And you can stop writing now, Jethro.

The interview ended at 7 minutes past the seventh hour.

Galilee
Sea Rescue

Jesus Ben Joseph
House of Simon Peter
Capernaum
Galilee

Dear Mr. Ben Joseph,

As you are probably aware, Galilee Sea Rescue is an organisation that exists to make the Sea of Galilee safe for both bathers and sailors. We have lifeguards situated at all the prime fishing and bathing locations around the lake and we have saved countless lives over the years. Which brings me to you, Mr. Ben Joseph.

I have been following your activities over the last few months – along with everyone else in Galilee – and I must say, I have been very impressed with all the reports I've heard. I have been tempted for some time to write to you concerning your unique gifts – especially regarding your ability to raise the dead. I don't need to tell you what an asset that would be in our line of work – it certainly beats CPR! It wasn't until last week, though, that I was convinced that you would be an ideal member of the GSR team.

According to the reports, you were seen last Tuesday, walking on the surface of the water all the way to the middle of the lake, where you met your disciples in their fishing boat. Then one of your disciples jumped out of the boat and started walking to you! Apparently, he wasn't quite as adept as you, as he started to sink, whereupon you strolled over and pulled him back out! I must say, Mr. Ben Joseph, the implications of this ability are huge for us at GSR. If you could teach our lifeguards to walk on water like you did, we could cut the time it takes to get to emergencies in half! All they would need to do is sprint across the waters, pluck the bathers out of trouble and carry them back to shore – what could be simpler?

I hope you will consider this opportunity very carefully, Mr. Ben Joseph. Walking around dusty towns day in, day out is all very well, but it must get a bit tiresome sometimes. If you joined GSR, you could enjoy the sea air and a life on the beach, knowing that you were keeping the shores of the Sea of Galilee safe from disaster. Think about it, Mr. Ben Joseph, and come and join the team.

Yours hopefully,

Benjamin Ben Benjamin
Director, Galilee Sea Rescue

The true identity of the tenth leper

TRANSCRIPT OF INTERVIEW

Messiah Candidate: Bartholomew of Jericho

Evidence of Messiahship: Alleged transformation of farm animals

Name of Witness: Caleb Ben Japheth

Occupation of Witness: Farm Hand

OBED: The interview begins at thirty-seven minutes past the fifth hour. I am Obed Ben Rabath and I am interviewing Caleb Ben Japheth. Caleb, what is your profession?

CALEB: I am a farm hand.

OBED: And who is your employer?

CALEB: My employer is Bartholomew of Jericho. Sheep farmer of note and Messiah to the People of God.

OBED: Why do you say he is the Messiah?

CALEB: I have seen him perform mighty miracles involving a variety of small farm animals.

OBED: When was this?

CALEB: This was just last week, sir. Wednesday, I believe.

OBED: And can you describe what you saw?

CALEB: Certainly. I was in the yard, sorting the horse manure when I saw a sheep.

OBED: Was that unusual?

CALEB: No, sir, it was not.

OBED: Is it relevant?

CALEB: Yes, sir, it is. I paid no heed to the sheep and went about my duties, but when I looked up again, the sheep had vanished and, in its place, there stood a cockerel.

OBED: A cockerel?

CALEB: Yes, sir. The sheep had miraculously turned into Spot, the cockerel.

OBED: I see, and what makes you think that this was the work of Bartholomew?

CALEB: Well, sir, as I was wondering at this strange occurrence, who should appear from behind the barn but Bartholomew himself. He was coming to collect his eggs.

OBED: Caleb, did it ever occur to you that the sheep simply walked away and the cockerel happened to be standing in its place?

CALEB: No, sir, it did not.

OBED: Or that your employer was simply in the vicinity because he needed some eggs?

CALEB: No, sir, that did not ever occur to me.

OBED: No, I don't suppose it did. Well, thank you for your time, Mr. Caleb, the Sanhedrin will certainly take your evidence into consideration when assessing Bartholomew's claim.

CALEB: Don't you want to hear about the goat that mooed like a cow?

OBED: That won't be necessary.

CALEB: Or the chicken that prophesied Bartholomew's glorious overthrowing of the Roman Empire?

OBED: No, thank you. Please go now. The interview is ended.

The interview ended at thirty-nine minutes past the fifth hour.

Camel Care For Beginners

Chapter 1 – *Buying Your Camel*

Welcome to the wonderful world of camels! These loveable beasts have formed the backbone of civilised societies for centuries. Their amazing stamina and ability to go without water for days have made them the perfect companion for any self-respecting desert dweller, and this little book will equip you with all the know-how you need to form the perfect partnership – you and your camel.

The first thing you need to know is how to go about purchasing your beast. Camel merchants visit most small villages on a regular basis. A good merchant should not only offer camels for sale but also all the extra equipment you will need. This includes a bucket, brush and sharp knife for grooming (see chapter two), a good supply of camel feed and a good, strong saddle. These are, of course, just the essentials. If you live near a city, however, you can find a good selection of camel markets, where just about every kind of camel accessory can be found. Some of the handier of these include hump warmers – for those cold desert nights, a discreet rope ladder for the more stubborn creatures and a specially designed turban, which, in the event of a sandstorm, can unwind into a shelter covering both you and your camel. Two pairs of special holes, punched into the side of the shelter, allow you to continue your journey undaunted - whatever the weather. (Shelters come in three different colour schemes.)

Your most important purchase, however, will, of course, be your camel. An important factor when choosing your animal is the age.

Don't buy anything younger than six months, as you run the risk of the camel 'adopting' you as its mother. When this happens, camels have been known to follow their owners everywhere. This can be very embarrassing for the owner and may eventually cause distress to the animal.

Another important factor is size. There is nothing more embarrassing than buying a camel and then finding that it is too large to mount. There is no real shame in being undersized, so be sensible with your purchase. Finally, the smell. This is a much overlooked factor when buying camels but remember, you will be spending a lot of time on this animal's back, so always ask yourself the question, 'Is this a smell I could live with?'

Once you have found your beast, do not try what some buyers have been known to do and walk round it, kicking its ankles to see if they are strong enough. You cannot find out anything useful by doing this and you risk being spat at by the camel – not to mention the camel merchant. Instead, simply engage in a little friendly bartering until you are both happy with the price, and the camel will be yours. All that is left is for the merchant to hand over the relevant documents and the reins and you will be free to ride away.

In the next chapter: *A clean camel is a happy camel: Grooming*

Jesus' miracles weren't popular with everyone

TRANSCRIPT OF INTERVIEW

Messiah Candidate: Jeremiah of Bethlehem

Evidence of Messiahship: Alleged vision

Name of Witness: Jeremiah of Bethlehem

Occupation of Witness: Shoemaker

OBED: The interview begins at the fourth hour. I am Obed Ben Rabath and I am interviewing Jeremiah of Bethlehem concerning a vision he claims to have received earlier this week. Jeremiah, could you tell me on which day you received the vision?

JEREMIAH: It was last Tuesday. I'm sure of that because I always make a point of buying a fresh loin of beef every Thursday to cast upon the waters of the lake. And my vision was definitely not on that day.

OBED: I see, and where were you, exactly?

JEREMIAH: I was in my shop. Making a beautiful pair of shoes for Caesar himself. He was due to call in that very afternoon to pick them up and I hadn't finished the soles.

OBED: Hmm. Could you describe the vision to me, please?

JEREMIAH: Yes, I could.

OBED: Would you describe the vision to me, please?

JEREMIAH: Certainly. As I hurried to complete the sole of Caesar's left shoe, I heard a noise so terrible that it made me scream like a small haddock in the very throes of death. Then, suddenly, the walls of my shop came crashing in and there stood a mighty herd of water buffalo, fresh from the hunt, gleaming yellow in the stark sunlight.

OBED: And what happened then?

JEREMIAH: The chief buffalo stepped forward and spoke in a voice that sounded like a thousand clay pots being dropped from a great height.

OBED: And what did he say?

JEREMIAH: "Rise up, Jeremiah, son of Jeremiah, maker of shoes, cutter of leather, eater of bread and collector of nice pebbles, for you are the Chosen One. You alone will overthrow the tyranny of Rome and restore the fortunes of Judah. Tread wisely, my son, and always floss after meals." Then, as suddenly as they had appeared, they were gone.

OBED: Right.

JEREMIAH: So when do I start?

OBED: Well, I have to send my report back to Sanhedrin Headquarters and they will weigh up the evidence. But be assured that, if they do decide that you are the Chosen One of God, I will be in touch with you straight away.

JEREMIAH: You do believe me, don't you?

OBED: Of course I do. Now, please leave.

JEREMIAH: You seem nervous.

OBED: Just excited.

JEREMIAH: Ah, of course. That's understandable. Well, until the next time, good and faithful servant, I bid you farewell.

OBED: Bye bye. Jethro, bolt the door.

The interview ended at five minutes after the fourth hour.

Greater Jerusalem Council

To: Zacchaeus
Chief Tax Collector
Jericho
Judea

Dear Mr. Zacchaeus,

I am writing to you concerning the unfortunate incident last week when you deemed it appropriate behaviour for a man of your stature (professionally speaking, that is, not physically — not that I'm saying you're small or anything) to climb one of the town's oldest and finest sycamore trees in order to see, of all things, a travelling preacher.

As the Chief Gardener of the entire Greater Jerusalem district, it is my responsibility to maintain all types of plant life in Jericho and I have to say that my job will be made considerably more difficult if members of the Jericho workforce think they can just use and abuse the trees at their own whim and convenience.

Normally, I would be forced to issue you with a 10 denarii fine for this misdemeanour but as you seem to have made a considerable U-turn in your company policy and given me a generous tax rebate, I am willing to overlook it this time. But please, Mr. Zacchaeus, in the future, get a stepladder.

Yours sincerely,

Josiah Ben Samuel
Chief Gardener, Greater Jerusalem Council

TRANSCRIPT OF INTERVIEW

Messiah Candidate: Jesus of Nazareth

Evidence of Messiahship: Alleged healing of blind man

Name of witnesses: Samuel Ben Hamin, Jeb the Lesser

Occupation of Witnesses: Beggars

OBED: The interview begins at the fifth hour. I am Obed Ben Rabath and I am interviewing Samuel Ben Hamin and his companion, Jeb, who would like to report an incident concerning Jesus of Nazareth. Samuel, what is your profession?

SAMUEL: Well, I was a beggar until recently.

OBED: And why was that?

SAMUEL: It was the only way I could make any money.

OBED: What was stopping you from getting a job?

JEB: This is Samuel the Blind.

OBED: What?

JEB: Samuel the Blind, sir.

OBED: Are you blind?

SAMUEL: No, sir. I can see perfectly well.

OBED: So why on earth are you called Samuel the Blind?

JEB: He *was* blind.

SAMUEL: That's right, sir - blind from birth.

JEB: I suppose we'll have to call you Samuel the *Was* Blind, now.

SAMUEL: Yes, I suppose you will.

OBED: What are you talking about!? How can you have been blind if you're not blind now? It's not like a cold, you know. You can't just take a couple of aspirins and stay in bed for a day or two. If you're blind, you're blind for good!

SAMUEL: Well, that's what I thought. I didn't think I'd ever see the light of day, but then this Jesus fellar turned up.

JEB: Ooh, he was lovely, sir; so polite.

OBED: And what exactly did he do?

SAMUEL: Well, I was just minding my own business, doing my usual spot of Saturday morning begging, when I heard some fellars talking about me.

OBED: What were they saying?

SAMUEL: They were asking this Jesus bloke whose fault it was that I was blind and he said that it wasn't anybody's fault. Well, I was just going to tell them that it was very rude to talk about people as if they weren't there when, all of a sudden, I heard someone spit on the ground and the next thing I knew, I was having mud smeared all over my eyes by a complete stranger.

OBED: Mud?

SAMUEL: That's right. Then he tells me to nip over to the Pool of Siloam and wash it all off again. Well, I'll tell you, sir, if someone had normally done that to me, they'd have felt the end of my stick, but there was something about his voice that made me want to do what he said.

OBED: And did you?

SAMUEL: Yep.

OBED: And what happened?

SAMUEL: As soon as I washed the mud off my eyes, I could see. It was incredible!

OBED: Are you trying to tell me that this Jesus character healed your blindness by smearing mud in your eyes?

SAMUEL: That's exactly what I'm trying to tell you.

OBED: That's ridiculous!

SAMUEL: What do you mean?

OBED: Well, if I was a doctor and a blind man asked me to heal him, I'm pretty sure that my first instinct would not be to reach for the mud! Whoever heard of such a thing?

SAMUEL: I suppose it does sound a bit strange, but...

OBED: It sounds more than strange, sonny, it sounds like a lie!

SAMUEL: What!?

OBED: Do you know what I think? I think you never were blind. I think you're making it all up!

JEB: No, sir. It's true. This really is Samuel the Was Blind!

OBED: Oh, shut up, will you! Nobody wants to know what you think!

JEB: Well!

OBED: And you – you ought to be ashamed of yourself – wasting Sanhedrin time like this! And to think I took you seriously!

SAMUEL: But it's true!

OBED: Enough! Get out of here! The interview is over. Smeared mud in your eyes – honestly.

The interview ended at four minutes past the fifth hour.

Candidates for Messiah

Name	Occupation	Reasons For	Reasons Against
Jeremiah of Bethlehem	Shoemaker	Received a vision of thirty-seven yellow water buffalo telling him to become the Messiah.	Clinically insane
Jason of Thebes	Merchant	Is willing to give 20% of anything he makes as the Messiah to the Sanhedrin.	Greek
John the Baptist	Baptist	Obviously some kind of prophet. Preaches repentance and brings hundreds back to God.	Dead
Rebekah of Bethel	Seamstress	Preaches the kingdom of God and gives generously to the work of the priests.	Female
Jesus of Nazareth	Carpenter	The blind see, the lame walk, the lepers are cured, the deaf hear, the dead are raised to life, and the Good News is being preached to the poor.	He didn't ask our permission
Bartholomew of Jericho	Farmer	Would quite like a change of scenery and thought he'd give being the Messiah a go.	Not really grasped the whole 'being the Messiah' concept
Zebudiah of Tyre	Tax Collector	Has a thorough knowledge of the scriptures and supports the Pharisees.	Tax Collector

Obed Ben Rabath
Pharisee and Sanhedrin
Galilean Representative
Will preside over weddings, funerals and bar mitzvahs

Dear Jacob,

As you can see from my report, I would have to say that the most likely candidate for the Messiah is Jesus of Nazareth. Even if you discount the somewhat dubious eye-witness reports of some of his so-called miracles, I cannot deny that the basic criteria for Messiahship, as laid out by the Sanhedrin, are all fulfilled in this man: the blind see, the lame walk, lepers are cured, the deaf hear, the dead are raised to life (yes, Jacob, I spoke to the dead girl myself), and the Good News is being preached to the poor. I can't see that we're going to find anyone who fits the bill any better.

Anyway, that's for you and the others to decide. Let me know what you think. But if you do decide against this Jesus chap, you might consider him for membership in the Sanhedrin. He seems very knowledgeable about the scriptures and he is certainly zealous for the People of God. I think he'd fit right in.

I look forward to hearing your decision. See you then.

Yours,

Obed

Dear Obed,

Have I taught you so little? Has the northern air dulled your mind so much that you can't see when you're being taken for a ride? I would expect the people of Galilee to be fooled by this Jesus character – they can hardly tell a Jew from a Greek up there, never mind recognise the Messiah - but frankly, Obed, I expected a little more insight from someone of your position.

The Jews are a gullible people, Obed. They'll believe anyone who offers them entertainment and a free drink. That's why we have always to have our wits about us. Oh, Jesus' credentials look good – the blind receive sight, the lame walk, the deaf hear – just the proof we've been looking for – but don't you see, Obed? That's just it! Jesus couldn't have done any of these things, because if he had, how would we be able to distinguish him from the real Messiah when he finally shows up?

I suppose it's an easy mistake to make for a rookie, so seeing as you're new to the Messiah-finding business, I'll overlook your recommendations this time; but really, Obed, I'm hoping for a big improvement next time.

Yours,

Jacob
(Pharisee-in-charge – Messianic division)

The Case of the Adulterous Dame

Allow me to introduce myself. My name's Mike Hammerstein and I'm a private investigator. Well, some poor Joe's gotta do it, so it may as well be me. I deal with the sleaze of society; the underbelly of Jerusalem's holy façade. You get to meet some interesting slime in my line of work – it ain't pretty but it pays the bills.

The afternoon in question was just like any other afternoon. The sun was shining through my office window so naturally my blinds were down. I'd had a few too many of the hard stuff the night before and my head was pounding. I guess I was drowning my sorrows – in my job you don't just have your own sorrows; you get to share other people's as well. Soon you got a mountain of the things and that takes some drowning.

So there I was, just finishing off the paperwork for my last assignment – *The Strange Case of the Maltese Pomegranate* – when there was a knock at the door and in walks a long-legged dame with a skirt she must have sprayed on that morning. It was Miss Cohen, my secretary. She handed me my mug of coffee and then told me there was someone waiting for me outside. I asked her to show them in. She turned to the door and hollered, "Come in!" I really needed to talk to her about her people skills.

In response to Miss Cohen's gentle invitation, in walked a guy. I was a little surprised, I admit. I'm used to slinky-looking dames slinking into my office and fluttering their pretty little eyelids at me, but I guess work was work. He was kinda average looking – average height, average build, average shoes – you get the picture. What struck me was his face – I could tell from his expression that something heavy was going down. He looked like he'd lost a denarius and found a sestertius. I offered him a seat and he took it. "This is Mr. Lewis," barked Miss Cohen, then she left, closing the door behind her.

We were alone. I just hoped he wasn't going to start fluttering his eyelids at me.

"What's the problem?" I asked. There's always a problem.

"It's my wife. I think she's being unfaithful."

It's always the same. "How can you tell?"

"She keeps doing herself up to the nines every evening, then she goes out and comes back in the morning all dishevelled and breathless."

"Maybe she's got a milk round?" – it was worth a try.

"I don't think so, Mr. Hammerstein."

"So, what do you want me to do about it?" I asked, knowing the answer.

"I want you to catch her red-handed."

"Are you sure about this?"

"Quite sure."

"My fees are simple. I need 200 up front, then 100 per morning up to the 5th hour when it goes up to 150 on account of the heat – then there's expenses, of course. They're extra."

"Agreed."

"When do we start?"

"Tonight. Meet me at the temple gates at the third watch."

"I'll be there."

"Oh, there'll be some Pharisees there as well – if she is being unfaithful, I may as well get the stoning over and done with as soon as possible."

Man, this guy was efficient. "I'll be there." He left the office and I was alone again.

A few hours later, I was standing at the temple gates feeling tired and cold. This was not my favourite time of the day. As far as I was concerned, mornings were for sleeping through. It wasn't long before I was surrounded by pharisees who couldn't wait to get started. One of them told me that they hadn't had a good stoning for over a week – they were getting excited. Eventually, Mr. Lewis arrived and we were ready.

It wasn't long before we found the house. My client had found his wife's little black book and we went from one address to the next, looking for the dame in question. We must have looked a strange mob. A P.I., a client and six holy men in dresses and boxes on their heads roaming round the back streets of Jerusalem was kind of unusual for the time of year.

Finally, we found the right place. I burst in through the front door and there was Mrs. Lewis and her friend. I can't say too much – it's a family show – but I could see they were enjoying each other's company.

Well, the scene after that was hectic to say the least. My client starting wailing and shouting at the top of his voice, the pharisees all leapt on Mrs. Lewis – if you ask me, they enjoyed that a little too much – and the guy she was with ran out of the door completely naked.
"What about him?" I shouted over the noise.
"What about him?" asked one of the pharisees.
"Well, it takes two to tango," I argued.
"Mr. Hammerstein, I may be a pharisee but I do know what these two were up to – and I can assure you it was not the tango. Excuse me."

And with that, they hauled the woman, half-naked, out of the house and down the street, singing, "There's going to be a stoning! There's going to be a stoning!" These guys really needed to get out more. Then one of them noticed some guy talking by the temple and they made for him like a lion on its prey.

When we got closer to him, I recognised him as Jesus. He was some new preacher sensation from Galilee who was supposed to do amazing miracles. In my line of work, you start to get a bit cynical about that kind of stuff, but I was curious what the pharisees were going to say to him.

"Jesus, stop talking and listen to us!" Well, that was a good start. It worked, though. The preacher turned and looked at the mob.
"We have just caught this woman in the act of adultery." There was an audible gasp from the crowd and people immediately started picking up stones, itching to throw them at the dame, who was just lying on the floor, shaking. "The law commands that we should stone such women. So how about it?"

Then every eye moved to Jesus, but he just stood there, playing with his stick, making patterns in the sand. After what seemed like hours, Jesus looked up at the crowd and said in a voice you wouldn't want to tangle with, "Let he who is without sin cast the first stone."

It was brilliant. Nobody knew what to do. People just looked at each other and then at Jesus, then at Mrs. Lewis, then just down at the ground. For the longest time, nobody did anything; then, one by one, they began to drop their stones and leave. The pharisees were the last to go, but even they could see they weren't going to get a stoning that day. I left with them and went back to the office, leaving Mrs. Lewis and Jesus alone.

When I got back, I just sat in my chair for I don't know how long and went over and over what had happened in my mind. Finally, I came to the conclusion that it was a good thing there weren't too many people around like Jesus, or I'd be out of a job.

The Daily Desert

- with the stories we want you to hear -

23rd February, 31AD

Mr Judas Iscariot
Iscariot Public Relations
Jerusalem

Dear Mr. Iscariot,

Thank you for your recent correspondence concerning your client, Mr. Jesus Bar Joseph. We have been very impressed with the accounts you have given of Jesus' amazing feats and we would like to send a photographer to follow you and your party for the duration of your tour of Judea. We have drawn up a programme of three events for your client to attend – each one will provide ample opportunity for him to demonstrate his talents and for you to gain maximum publicity. The programme is as follows:

Venue One - *Ephraim*

There will be an important, high-profile wedding feast in Ephraim on the first Saturday in March. We have spoken to the feast organisers and they have agreed to pay five shekels for every jar of water Jesus turns into wine. The wine must, of course, be of the highest quality or we risk a fight breaking out.

We were also wondering if Jesus might agree to some other, similar, transformations, such as pebbles into pineapple chunks or vermin into vol-au-vents – that sort of thing. Obviously, the organisers would need to know of any such plans in advance to avoid over-catering.

We will, of course, want shots of Jesus shaking hands with the families and perhaps giving a blessing to the happy couple. That sort of thing always goes down well with the readers.

Venue Two – *Jericho*

The Jericho town council have given the go-ahead for us to set up a large tent in the middle of the town. We can set up a stage and bring in a local choir to warm up the audience before Jesus rises up amidst smoke and trumpet blasts through a trap door in the stage. We then bring on a long line of sick people who will all be healed by Jesus. Of course, we must make sure that none of the sick people have ugly diseases such as leprosy or missing limbs, as these do not make for good pictures.

We are hoping for considerable sponsorship support for this event and we predict there will also be a lot of fringe activities such as circus performers, camel rides and hot dog stands; all of which mean extra revenue for us.

Venue Three – *Bethany*

There is a large house situated to the south of Bethany, owned by a wealthy camel merchant. He has agreed to let us use his swimming pool in return for a bit of free publicity. We would like Jesus to walk across the pool a few times so that we can get some pictures. It might be nice then if one of his followers could join him on the water and perhaps do a little dance to give the story a bit of a novelty angle – Jesus relaxing with his friends – though there may be health and safety issues which would need to be worked out first.

We are confident you and your client will agree that these three events, placed side by side and accompanied by a substantial advertising campaign, will greatly enhance both your client's profile and his popularity. If we are to go ahead with these plans, however, there will be one or two loose ends that need tying up.

First of all, there must be very clear boundaries set for where Jesus can and cannot go. We are referring, of course, to your recent detour through Samaria whilst travelling to Judea. This, in itself, was an unwise decision but we now hear that Jesus actually started a conversation with a Samaritan woman. If word of this incident were to leak out, your client would struggle to get a booking at a children's birthday party. It goes without saying that if an incident like this were to happen again, The Daily Desert would be forced to cut all ties with Iscariot Public Relations and its clients.

In addition to this, we have heard about a botched preaching engagement in the hills above the Sea of Galilee. Apparently, thousands of people were stranded miles from anywhere without any food. This is just the sort of disastrous planning which we at The Daily Desert are eager to avoid. Fortunately for you, your client was able to use one of his tricks to turn the situation into positive publicity, but you should never have been in that mess in the first place. Careful planning and flawless execution are vital if events such as the ones outlined above are to succeed, Mr. Iscariot. We believe you have learnt your lesson and trust that no such problems will arise in the future.

We trust that these proposals will be met with yours and your client's satisfaction. If you have any queries, please do not hesitate to get in touch with us, otherwise, a representative of the paper will meet with you in Ephraim to run through all the details. We look forward to meeting you, Mr. Iscariot. Your enthusiasm for your client is infectious – he is fortunate to have such a loyal associate at his side.

Yours sincerely,

Joseph Ben Jehosaphat
Editor, The Daily Desert

Iscariot
Public
Relations

Portfolio

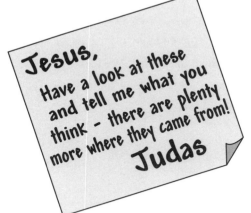

Jesus,
Have a look at these
and tell me what you
think – there are plenty
more where they came from!
Judas

Call Judas on 846253 for details.
Iscariot Public Relations
We're here to help.

Fishermen

Are you tired of missing a day of fishing because of storms?

Surfers

Have you spent too many hours waiting for the waves to come?

Then <u>Jesus</u> could be just the man for <u>you</u>!

There's nothing more frustrating than having to sit around and wait for a storm to pass before you can go out on the lake and earn an honest day's wage catching fish. Or perhaps you've spent all morning waxing up your surfboards and carried them down to the beach, only to find that the lake is like a millpond. Well, you don't have to be frustrated any longer, now that Jesus of Nazareth is here! Jesus has already built up a great reputation as a preacher and healer, but did you know he can also control the very wind and the rain? It's true! Just the other day, Jesus and his disciples were caught in the middle of a terrible storm whilst fishing on the lake. Even the experienced hands of the fishermen couldn't keep the boat afloat for much longer – they were in big trouble! Or so they thought! As soon as Jesus realised the danger, he leapt up and, with a mighty cry, commanded the wind and the rain to cease. And they did!
And for just 5 silver coins per half day, they will for you, too!
Just let him know what you want – calm for fishing or breakers the size of trees for surfing – and Jesus will just say the word.
It's as simple as that!

Call Judas on 846253 for details.
Iscariot Public Relations
We're here to help.

Mums

Don't know what to buy your child for his birthday?

Look no further!

The amazing

Jesus® Action Figure

is the perfect gift!

The amazing Jesus® Action Figure is quite simply the
best toy in the world!
Standing 12" high, and featuring fantastic Moving Arm®
Technology, your child won't ever ask for another toy again!
Using the latest Moving Arm® Technology, you can make Jesus' arm
crash down on the tables of the Temple moneychangers* (can also
be used for laying hands on the sick[†])!
Each Action Figure comes with accessories too! The amazing Flip
Action® wine glasses are filled with clear water one minute, but
with a simple twist of the handle, they're filled with wine!
Why not collect all twelve Disciple Action Figures® as well and
make your collection complete!

Jesus® Action Figures

They're the perfect gift for all the family!

* Moneychangers' tables sold separately
† Sick Action Figures sold separately

Call Judas on 846253 for details.
Iscariot Public Relations
We're here to help.

The Judean
Tourist Association

Mr. and Mrs. Sedgwick

30 Olive Tree Crescent

Gaza

Judea

JU12 6HK

Dear Mum and Dad,

It's brilliant staying with Uncle Peter. He let me go fishing the other day but he said not to tell you.

He's got a friend called Jesus who goes around healing people and telling them about God - I think you'd like him. Yesterday, we went to see some friends of his, but one of them had died, but Jesus healed him - after he'd been dead for four days! And he didn't smell or anything! There was a big party afterwards. It was brilliant! See you soon.

Lots of love,
Tobias

Picture: *Bethany Synagogue*

Goldstein & Sons
Insurance Agents

16th February, 33AD

To: Lazarus Smith
Bethany

Dear Mr. Smith,

Thank you for your recent correspondence regarding a claim on the policy you took out with Goldstein & Sons in June 28AD. Although we are committed to providing for our customers in times of crisis with a minimum of fuss, we do feel that your particular circumstance is somewhat unorthodox and we regret to inform you that we feel we must deny your claim. Our reason for this decision is as follows:

The main prerequisite of a life insurance claim is that the policyholder is, in fact, dead. In the whole of this company's history, we have never had a life insurance claim made by the policyholder. We have your most recent medical records to hand and they confirm that you are very much alive. We are not inferring that what you say in your letter is false – it is not for us to judge our customers' honesty or, indeed, sanity – but even if you *were* dead for four days, you yourself claim in your letter to be 'feeling a lot better now'. With regard to your other enquiry, it may surprise you to hear, Mr. Smith, that we do not operate a no-claims bonus scheme with our life insurance policies.

I hope you are not too disappointed with this decision. I can assure you that we will be more than happy to make good your claim once your death is of a more permanent nature. If there is anything else we can help you with, please don't hesitate to contact us.

Yours sincerely,

Jacob Goldstein
Director, Goldstein & Sons

Solomon & Schwartz Solicitors

24th February, 33AD

To: **Jacob Goldstein**
       Goldstein & Sons

Dear Mr. Goldstein,

I am writing to you on behalf of my client, Mr. Lazarus Smith. You may recall that Mr. Smith wrote to you on February 3rd, requesting the money promised to him by your company on the event of his death. You replied to this letter on February 16th with a refusal to pay, based on the fact that my client was not dead. Upon close examination of the policy agreement that Mr. Smith received from you, I am in no doubt that Goldstein & Sons is in breach of contract.

Your claim that my client is ineligible on the basis that he is alive is irrelevant. Your policy agreement clearly states that the agreed amount will be paid on the occasion of the policyholder's death. The agreement does not say that this payment will be withheld should the policyholder recover from his/her state of non-life. There are a great deal of eyewitnesses who can testify that my client was, indeed, dead and should, therefore, be entitled to claim on his life insurance. It is not the fault of my client that your company did not foresee such a reversal of fortune.

Should you still wish to contest my client's claim, I will be happy to accompany you to the court of the Roman governor, Pontius Pilate. In the mean time, perhaps you should consider speaking to the man responsible for my client's miraculous recovery – one Jesus of Nazareth. Be prepared to wait in line, though. There's a long list of wine makers, caterers, crutch suppliers, roofing contractors and undertakers who wish to speak to him first. I look forward to hearing from you.

Yours sincerely,

Benjamin Schwartz

Solicitor, Solomon & Schwartz Solicitors

Dear Mum and Dad,

We had a brilliant day today! We were going into Jerusalem with Jesus for the Passover and suddenly loads of people started cheering him and throwing their coats down and waving palm leaves at him. Some Pharisees tried to stop them but Jesus told them off!

Everyone's really excited now because they think Jesus is going to become king! Just think - I might know a king! Don't worry - I'll get him to invite you to the palace.

Lots of love,
Tobias

Mr. and Mrs. Sedgwick

30 Olive Tree Crescent

Gaza

Judea

JU12 6TK

Picture: *Jerusalem from the Mount of Olives*

Polite Notice

Would the residents of Jerusalem please refrain from using palm leaves to welcome potential kings of Israel into the city. I have personally invested a great deal of time and effort into nurturing these trees from saplings through to maturity and was not, therefore, overly thrilled to find them stripped bare and the leaves strewn all over the place in an act of wanton vandalism. In the future, if you must wave plants at visiting VIPs, please use dandelions.

Thank you very much.

Josiah Ben Samuel
(Chief Gardener, Greater Jerusalem Council)

Visitors' Guide

Welcome!
On behalf of the people of Jerusalem, the Greater Jerusalem Council welcomes you to our wonderful city!

There is so much to see and visit here, you probably won't be able to take it all in with one visit – but this specially produced leaflet will hopefully point you in the right direction. Why not try some of these suggestions for size?

Herod's Temple
Also known as the Temple of God, this incredible structure will take your breath away!

Never before has there been such beauty, such craftsmanship, such power in one building. Oh yes, you can point to the great architectural feats of the Romans, the Greeks and the Egyptians and yes, some of them are very big and impressive – but none quite match up to Jerusalem's finest accomplishment!

Ever since the destruction of Solomon's temple over 500 years ago, it has been the goal of every Jew to see the temple reinstated. But only King Herod the Great had the vision, the courage and the money to make it happen.

50 years on and still it is not yet complete – but already the grandeur of this mighty place of worship is supremely evident. Jews from all over the ancient world are invited to take in the splendour, the wonder and the sheer opulence that is – Herod's Temple!

The Mount of Olives
No visit to Jerusalem is complete without a gentle walk up the wonderfully picturesque Mount of Olives.

No one is quite sure how this magnificent mountain, covered in olive groves, got its name, but everyone is agreed it is a delightful place to visit, offering a breathtaking view of the city.

The Garden of Gethsemane
And while you're there, why not visit the Garden of Gethsemane? A favourite with both friends and lovers alike, the peace and tranquillity of this slice of paradise is sure to sooth your senses. There's many a happy moment to be had there – so don't miss it!

The Temple Market
Whatever it is you're looking for – whether it's a sheep to sacrifice or a straw camel to take home for Granny – the Temple Market has it all!

Beginning only four years ago, the market has already established itself as <u>the</u> place to visit for all your household needs.

Suitable for all the family, there is a food square in the centre of the market, offering foods from all over the ancient world. There's something to suit every taste here!

These suggestions are just a few of the thousands of exciting things to do at the greatest city on earth – Jerusalem!

Notice to All Prophets

Please note that the fig trees in this area are the property of the Greater Jerusalem Council. It is, therefore, an offence to curse, bemoan, slander or generally badmouth the trees in any way. Anyone found cursing the fig trees will be fined 3 silver coins and ordered off the land.

Josiah Ben Samuel
(Chief Gardener, Greater Jerusalem Council)

The Temple of God

Gift Voucher

30 Silver Coins

This voucher entitles the bearer to goods worth up to 30 silver coins bought from any stall at the temple market or from the temple gift shop.

Presented to ...*Judas Iscariot*...

On the occasion of ...*betraying his best friend,*...............
...*Jesus, to the authorities.*.............................

Words from the Wise

Friday, May 15th

Aries - Mar 21 – Apr 19

A small hole in your socks may be just the excuse you've been looking for to switch careers. Don't tell the boss till Tuesday, though!

Lucky Camel: Walter

Taurus - Apr 20 – May 20

Mars is in the ascendancy this week so you should try to keep away from blood-crazed barbarians as much as possible.

Lucky vegetable: Turnip

Gemini - May 21 – Jun 21

An unusual wobble in Saturn's orbit means that Geminis should stay indoors all week. You can't be too careful with planetary wobbles.

Unlucky herb: Arsenic

Cancer - Jun 22 – Jul 22

If a stranger turns up on the doorstep selling tangerines this week, bolt the doors – tangerine season isn't for another month!

Lucky word: Perpendicular

Leo - July 23 – Aug 22

No amount of rubbing is going to get rid of that sore, so you might as well learn to love it. Just don't let the rabbi see it.

Unlucky weather: Tornado

Virgo - Augt 23 – Sep 22

An unusually shaped haddock will mark the beginning of a strange journey into the unknown. Don't forget to pack your sandwiches.

Lucky uncle: Gordan

Libra - Sep 23 – Oct 22

The passing of a previously unseen comet across the path of Mercury this week has no lasting significance for your life whatsoever.

Unlucky sandwich: Tuna and sweetcorn

Scorpio - Oct 23 – Nov 21

An axe man will turn up at your door on Wednesday night intent on killing you and your household. Otherwise a fairly uneventful week.

Lucky cloud: Cumulus Nimbus

Sagittarius - Nov 22 – Dec 21

An intriguing package promises to lead to romance on Monday – until you realise it is addressed to your next-door neighbour.

Unlucky amphibian: Newt

Capricorn - Dec 22 – Jan 19

Try to steer away from large wooden objects this week – they will only lead to trouble. Trust no one – except perhaps your mother.

Unlucky empire: Roman

Aquarius - Jan 20 – Feb 18

You feel on top of the world this week; ready for anything. You feel you could take on the whole world armed only with a smile – don't.

Lucky utensil: Potato masher

Pisces - Feb 19 – Mar 20

You might *think* that covering yourself with oil and running naked around the city will help things, but it will only make them worse.

Unlucky torture: Thumbscrew

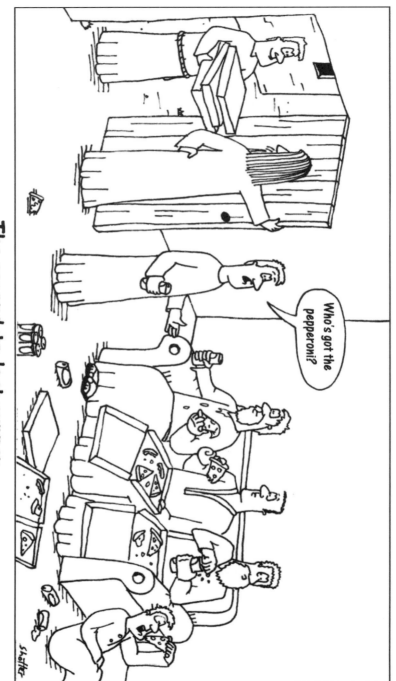

The second-to-last supper

'The Last Supper'
Menu

Appetizer
Bitter Herbs Mousse
and Toast

Main Course
Roast Lamb

Dessert
Unleavened Bread
broken and served with
Red Wine

Please feel free to sit wherever you like. Except Judas. A special seat has been reserved for you next to the door. Please stay seated at the end of your meal, as Jesus wishes to say a few words.
We hope you enjoy your evening.

Northerners – "Common As Muck!"

There was an ugly scene early this morning in the high priest's courtyard, involving a Galilean fisherman known as Simon Peter.

Whilst warming himself beside a fire, one of the girls on duty there tried to make conversation with him.

"We'd just had a prisoner brought in for questioning who came from Galilee," commented the girl. "It was that preacher bloke – you know – Jesus. Well, as soon as I heard this other fellar speak, I knew he was from up north as well, so I says to him, 'Are you with that Jesus bloke?' – just making small talk, like, and he just snapped at me – 'No!'. Charming, I thought. Anyways, I knew he was from Galilee and it couldn't have been a coincidence, so I said to him, 'I know you're from Galilee – you must be with him', but he nearly bit my head off that time – 'I am not with Jesus!' he shouted.

"Then Nathan, a mate of mine, came up to see if he was bothering me and when he saw who it was, he said, 'I recognise you – you're mates with that preacher bloke, aren't you?' Well, that was it. He just blew his nut! Thankfully, his northern accent became so thick that I could barely understand what he was shouting, but I don't think it was very nice. Nathan was quite upset by the whole episode – and in the high priest's courtyard, as well. Then the cock crowed and he just stopped for a moment, had a little sort of wobble and then ran off into the darkness, blubbing. He was a right nutter, if you ask me.

"It just goes to show, though – you try to be nice to northerners – what with them being northern and all – and they just throw it back in your face. They're common as muck, the lot of 'em."

It is not clear what happened to Simon Peter, but there were no other incidents reported. However, if you do come across an oversized northerner smelling of fish and sobbing uncontrollably, you are advised to give him a wide berth.

'Ear' Miss for Temple Guard

In a related incident, there are reports of strange goings on in the Garden of Gethsemane on the Mount of Olives.

Whilst arresting the preacher, Jesus of Nazareth, last night, Malchus, a temple security guard, had a run in with one of Jesus' followers.

"It was quite dark so I didn't get a good look at him", said Malchus, "but from what I could make out, he seemed to be an oversized northerner smelling of fish."

According to witnesses, the unidentified follower pulled out a sword and leapt at Malchus shouting, "Run, Jesus, run!" and before Malchus could react, the attacker had hacked off his left ear.

Malchus was heard to shout, "Ow! That really hurt!"

Chaos was about to break out when Jesus, who had not taken the assailant's advise, bent down and picked up the severed ear. Then, having wiped off the dirt on his sleeve, he apparently stuck it back on to Malchus's head, healing the guard instantly.

"It's true," confirmed the two-eared Malchus. "I couldn't believe it – one minute I've got the mother of all earaches and the next minute I'm fine."

With his ear restored to full health, Malchus was then able to arrest Jesus and take him in for questioning. As for the mystery ear slicer, he escaped in the confusion and is still at large.

"If I ever get hold of him, it won't be just his ear I'll be cutting off," commented Malchus.

Luke 22:47-51

Jesus' razor-sharp wit diffused what was rapidly becoming a tense situation

Polite Notice

Please note that the Garden of Gethsemane is the property of the Greater Jerusalem Council. As such, it is an offence to hold any kind of military operation on this site. That means no angry mobs, no lynching, and absolutely no severing and subsequent littering of any part of the human anatomy. This garden exists for the enjoyment of everyone and it did not grow itself. Many hours of tender, loving care have gone into it and I would be grateful, therefore, if any future twilight arrests could be carried out elsewhere.

Thank you very much.

Josiah Ben Samuel
(Chief Gardener, Greater Jerusalem Council)

Marcus
Have bit of a problem stop Jews getting restless again stop
Want me to crucify a preacher stop
Pilate

Pilate
So what's the problem stop
Marcus

Marcus
Preacher seems all right stop Hasn't done anything wrong
stop Just a bit odd stop
Pilate

Pilate
Tell Jews to bog off stop You are the governor stop
Marcus

Marcus
Have sorted it out stop Said no way stop Washed my hands
of it stop
Pilate

Pilate
Good thinking stop So when are you crucifying him stop
Marcus

Marcus
This afternoon stop
Pilate

Passover Feast a "roaring success"

This year's Passover Feast is set to be one of the best ever according to Caiaphas, the High Priest.

"The Passover is the high point of the calendar every year," commented Caiaphas, "but this year, there seems to be a real party atmosphere."

As usual, Jerusalem has opened its gates to thousands of visitors who have been arriving over the past few days. Caiaphas was confident that there would be no trouble, despite the large crowds, although Governor Pilate has expressed security concerns. "I have assured Pilate we are here to honour our God, not to fight," said Caiaphas, earlier today.

There's still time to make a sacrifice!

Don't worry if you haven't had time to make a Passover sacrifice yet. The temple will be open until sunset tonight and extra priests have been brought in to cope with the increased demand. All kinds of guaranteed kosher beasts can still be purchased from the temple market at special feast prices. So don't delay – get yourself down to the temple now and make that sacrifice. It's an affordable way to keep guilt at bay. You know it makes sense!

Court in Brief

Jethro Ben Jared arrested – drunk in charge
Asa Ben Eliakim arrested – in possession of a deadly weapon
Azor Ben Jotham crucified – breaking and entering
Jesus Ben Joseph crucified – civil unrest
Joram Ben Eliud crucified – grand theft equestrian

Radio Jerusalem

Broadcasting to the whole of the ancient world

Transcript of voxpops from bystanders at Golgotha, concerning the death of Jesus of Nazareth. For use in the Sunday morning talk show.

"It's a terrible thing – they should never have crucified him. He was such a nice man."
Mrs. D. Berber, Bethany

"I've lost all faith in the Sanhedrin – after what they did to that lovely man."
Mrs S. Baigel, Jerusalem

"Well, he must have done something very bad. They don't nail people up on crosses for nothing, you know."
Mr. R. Goodman, Jerusalem

"I think we may have made a mistake."
A. Centurion, Jerusalem

"Crucify him! Crucify him!"
"They have crucified him."
"Have they? Oh, righty ho. I'll be off, then."
Mr. T. Rosen, Bethlehem

"Is that it? I was expecting him to jump off the cross and beat all the Romans up or something. What an anticlimax."
Mrs. B. Weinberg, Capernaum

"I'm not quite sure what he's up there for, but I have complete faith in the Sanhedrin. They're always right – they have God on their side, don't they?"
Mrs. T. Segal, Jericho

"Wasn't he the fellar we were all waving palm leaves at last week?"
Mr. P. Samuels, Jerusalem

The Judean
Tourist Association

Mr. and Mrs. Sedgwick

30 Olive Tree Crescent

Gaza

Judea

JU12 6HK

Dear Mum and Dad,
I want to come home. The Romans
have crucified Jesus. He was arrested
last night when he was with Uncle
Peter and his friends and they took
him to see Pilate and then all the
people who were waving palm leaves
at him last week were all shouting for
him to die and then they crucified
him this afternoon. Everyone's really
upset. Uncle Peter seems more upset
than anyone. I really wanted you to
meet Jesus. I think you would have
liked him.

Lots of love,
Tobias

Picture: *Herod's Temple*

The Daily Damnation

It's a hell of a paper!

Friday, May 15th

GOTCHA

It's official - Jesus Christ is dead! Great celebrations are already underway as Hell revels in its most historic victory ever! The Daily Damnation was honoured earlier today with a statement from the Dark Lord himself:

"Jesus has been to us a tiresome thorn in the flesh, presuming to stand against my kingdom and, in doing so, inflicting a great many casualties among our ranks. Our darkest minds have been working relentlessly, trying to find some weakness in this infuriating adversary. I even spoke to him myself in an attempt to win his soul. Anyone else would have crumbled in my presence but this insolent upstart would not yield.

"This irritation has, I confess, made me a little touchy of late and I do apologise most insincerely to those who have borne the brunt of my anger. I realise that having one's head ripped off and thrown into the abyss is not the best way to start the week, but I have been under a lot of stress lately. "I know that you will not hold it against me, though, for I and I alone have brought fabulous glory to this most inglorious kingdom. For at our darkest hour, when we had almost given up all hope of victory, this so-called 'King of Kings' was murdered in a wicked and shameful manner. He hung from a cursed cross and suffered the humiliation of a crowd made up of the most joyously evil band of servants we could muster. But the most delightful thing about it was that it was all so easy. This 'champion' who had caused us such despicable grief up till then, suddenly became the most feeble of prey. It was almost as if he allowed himself to be beaten! But, of course, no one would ever go through such pain willingly. It was all my doing. I have conquered! I am king! I can never be beaten!"

We are very grateful for this statement and would like to pass on our congratulations to the Dark Lord for a job well done.

Day of the Living Dead!

The excitement of the Passover celebrations was overshadowed yesterday by the alleged appearance of a number of dead people walking through the streets of Jerusalem.

Reports have been coming in from all over the city of sightings of the long-dead corpses. Jeremiah Benmohel, a bread shop owner and eyewitness, said he saw two dead people enter his shop at about the tenth hour. "They walked in and asked me if I had any haddock," explained Mr. Benmohel. "When I told them it was a bread shop they just apologised and left. I knew they were dead because my cousin Jabel died last year and they smelt just the same."

Details are sketchy but we can confirm that all the sightings so far have been of dead holy people. Rabbis, priests, prophets and teachers have all been spotted.

The oldest reported corpse belongs to Jebediah Goodman – a well-known local mystic who died 143 years ago of an inflated tongue. His last words were probably among his most wise – but they were unfortunately rendered incomprehensible by his strange complaint.

The Temple has issued the following statement concerning the bizarre appearances:

"The Temple priests have been made aware of several dead people walking the streets of Jerusalem, conversing with the people.

This, coupled with the unusual darkness which occurred immediately prior to the sightings and the mysterious rending in half of the sanctuary curtain, have been taken as a message from the Lord God himself. As yet, however, we are unsure exactly what that message is."

Meanwhile, the corpses are slowly being gathered up and led to their (hopefully) final resting place.

Health and safety experts have advised the general public not to approach a dead person themselves, as one touch can result in ritual uncleanness for up to one week. The safest course of action is to wait for a trained corpse whisperer to remove the danger using specially sanctified clothing and equipment.

Weather Report

The weather today will be dry and hot. Just like yesterday and probably just like tomorrow. Hot, hot, hot. And dry. Let's not forget dry. Yes, sir, hot and dry is what it's gonna be. So don't forget your sun cream.

Stilman's Luxury Cemeteries

Don't spend eternity with anyone less

Mrs. D. Lubovich
16 East Street
Jerusalem

Dear Mrs. Lubovich,

Thank you very much for your letter dated Monday, May 18th, concerning the unfortunate events of Passover week. First of all, I would like to convey my sincere apologies for any distress caused by the news. Believe me, there was no one more surprised than me to hear that some of our late customers had left their resting places and were walking the streets of Jerusalem. Why anyone, dead or undead, would ever want to leave one of our luxury tombs is beyond me. Which brings me to your husband.

It is, of course, perfectly natural to want to know whether one's loved ones are still at rest, where one left them, or whether they have joined the ranks of the undead – wandering the streets – not alive and yet not truly at rest. The thought of such a fate befalling a loved one would surely be unbearable.

And that's why, Mrs. Lubovich, I am happy to be able to tell you that reports of our clients' resurrections have been greatly exaggerated. It appears that only the corpses of *holy* people were revived and I am pleased to report, therefore, that your beloved Leon is still very much dead, safely tucked away in his eternal sanctuary.

Now that I have been able to put your mind at rest, I'd like to take this opportunity to make you an incredible offer. Due to the unusual events of

May 15th, a selection of our luxury properties have suddenly become available at a ridiculously low price. There are no forms to fill in, no medical is necessary and no salesman will call - and remember, you **do not** have to occupy your tomb at the time of purchase. All you have to do is pay the massively discounted ownership fee and your Stilman's Luxury Tomb will be ready and waiting for you as soon as you need it, leaving you with one less thing to worry about.

I'll be ready to go over the details with you as soon as you realise what a great opportunity this is. And don't forget, Mrs Lubovich – if you introduce a friend to Stilman's Luxury Cemeteries, I'll knock off an extra 10%!

PLUS If you respond to this letter within 10 days you'll receive a beautiful carriage clock absolutely free!

I know I'll be seeing you soon, Mrs. Lubovich, so until then, shalom!

Joel Stilman
Managing Director, Stilman's Luxury Cemeteries

Thursday, May 7th

There is unrest amongst the flock. The humans' Passover festival is drawing near and already Cuthbert, Barbara and Percival have been taken away to be sacrificed. For days now, our food supply has been increasing and the flock have been lapping it up like idiots. I try to warn them but they just follow one another like, well, sheep. I fear the worst.

Friday, May 8th

Gordon and Celeste have been taken away. Poor Celeste. First there was the incident with the stuffed artichoke and now this. She really deserved better. It seems so unfair that we have to take the blame for what humans have done. Don't they realise they can use bulls for sin offerings too? Who am I kidding? Bulls are far too expensive for sacrificing – and we are only sheep after all.

Saturday, May 9th

A crowd of humans came by today to listen to someone speak. I would have ignored them but I heard him mention something about sheep. I grazed as close to him as I could without looking conspicuous and listened in. He was telling a story about a sheep who got lost. The shepherd in the story left the flock and went off to look for the lost sheep. When he found it, he brought it back to the flock and threw a party for all his friends. Sounds like a nutter if you ask me.

Sunday, May 10th

Had a nasty bout of wind today.

Monday, May 11th

That human was round here again this morning. He seems to be called Jesus. He said something that I found very disturbing. He told the people with him that he was the Lamb of God! It's all very suspicious. My guess is he's trying to pretend that he's a sheep so that he can take even more of us for his barbaric Passover festival. The depths these humans will stoop to. Still, he'll have to disguise himself a bit better. Not even Stanley would be fooled by a two-legged, non-woolly sheep.

Tuesday, May 12th

Stanley's been taken. I've sent Doreen and Eric out to spy on the human they call Jesus. If he's up to something, we need to know what it is.

Wednesday, May 13th

No sign of Doreen and Eric.

Thursday, May 14th

Still no sign.

Friday, May 15th

It's been a strange day. The sky went black for three hours this afternoon. There was an eerie silence and no one dared bleat. The darkness eventually passed, but the strange feeling didn't. None of the flock touched their food this evening. I can't help worrying about Doreen and Eric. I've still had no word from them and I'm beginning to think I never will.

Saturday, May 16th

The whole flock have been wandering about the fields in silence. Even the birds have stopped singing. There's a heaviness in the air, as if something terrible has happened, but no one's quite sure what. There is some good news though - Doreen and Eric are safe. They arrived back late this evening. I plan to speak with them first thing tomorrow.

Sunday, May 17th

I woke early this morning feeling much better. The heaviness has lifted and there's a feeling of anticipation in the air. I went straight round to Doreen and Eric's patch to find out what news they had and was greeted by a very excited Eric. It took a while to find out what had happened, as they were both bleating faster than I could follow, but I eventually gathered that the human, Jesus, had been arrested soon after they had started spying on him.

They went on to tell me how he had been sacrificed! Jesus – a human – sacrificed! Of course, when they told me that this had taken place on a hill outside Jerusalem, on a cross – and by Roman soldiers – I didn't believe it. It couldn't have been a sacrifice ~ it wasn't kosher! I tried to explain this to them, but they were too excited to listen.

Well, at least we survived the Passover ~ that's more than can be said for him.

Lamb of God, indeed; what will they think of next?

Calling all sheep!

Do you think you have the raw end of the deal?
Are you tired of living in fear of being sacrificed?
Well, fear no more because we have

Good News!

At long last, humans have found someone
spotless enough to die in our place!
Yes, it true!
Jesus of Nazareth – also known as the <u>Lamb of God</u> –
had done nothing wrong – ever – and yet he allowed
himself to be killed in order to free lambs from the
tyranny of sacrifice. It is not yet known why a human
would want to do such a thing –
but all that matters is that we have been liberated!

Jesus died to set lambs free!

So now is the time to rise up, fellow sheep, and join us
as we spread the good news of Jesus!
We'll go through all Jerusalem, Judea and Samaria –
and to the ends of the earth – proclaiming salvation to
all lambs through Jesus Christ!

Hallelujah!

Kevin,
This is it!
This is the big time!
Gordan

The
HEAVENLY
HOST

MEMO

To: Gordan and Kevin, Angels in Training
From: Gabriel

All right, lads, listen up. I have great news. You have been chosen to be the first ones to tell the good news about Jesus to the humans! I hope you realise what an honour this is for you; plus, if you get this right, you might just get to be fully-fledged angelic beings!

So here's the plan: You will be posted at the empty tomb to wait for Mary Magdalene to turn up, and when she does, you tell her to go away. Of course, you don't just say, 'Go away, Mary' – obviously you have to be nice about it, but that's the basic idea. And in case you were wondering, you can't just save yourselves the wait and go round to Mary's house and tell her. The Lord thought it would be a nice idea for Mary to see the empty tomb for herself. You know what he's like – he's always had a flair for the dramatic.

Anyway, I know you're just trainee angels, so I thought I'd give you some pointers about what to say and what not to say – I've got a feeling this encounter might be going in the new book, so you need to get it just right. See what you think.

Possible lines:

Hasn't he used that one before?

"Greetings, Mary, blessed among women." ←

"Shalom! and welcome to the empty tomb!"

"Why do you come here looking for Jesus when, ← *Boring!*
in fact, he's not here but elsewhere?"

"Why do you look for the living among the dead?" ← *I like this one – very poetic!*

Definite no-no lines:

"Hello, Mary. Look, I'm sorry to disappoint you, ← *What's wrong with this?*
but I'm afraid Jesus isn't here. So you may as
well go home. Bye!"

"He's not here!"

"Beat it, Blubface!" ← *Subtle – I like it!*

Hope these are some help. Don't mess this up, lads. The whole world is watching. No pressure, though. See you at the party!

Gabriel

See you down there!
Gordan

The Daily Damnation

It's a hell of a paper!

Sunday, May 17th

AAAAARRGH!

The underworld has today been reeling from what some are describing as the worst disaster to befall the Dark Lord since his fall from grace. Jesus Christ - Hell's most hated enemy - is alive!

It was only Friday when the Son of God was dying a slow and painful death on a cross outside Jerusalem. Celebrations were still going strong in Hell a day later when, seemingly out of nowhere, Jesus – no longer in chains but in full battle dress and wielding a two-edged sword sharper than a very sharp thing – stormed the gates and slaughtered thousands of dark angels. He then strode through the dungeons, setting the prisoners free and mercilessly butchering any demons that crossed his path.

In a final onslaught, he hunted down the Dark Lord himself and stole that which was most dear to him – the keys to death and hell!

Those left standing in the aftermath of this attack were

shocked and appalled.

Three separate reporters have been sent to get a statement from the Dark Lord – none have returned.

All that is left to do now is clean up the mess and get on with our afterlives. This turn of events will be a major setback for the Dark Lord – one from which he may never recover – but one thing is certain, he may have lost the war but there are plenty of battles left to win.

Weather Report

The weather in hell will be fairly cool today with temperatures falling as low as $8,373\,°c$. Don't be deceived, however, you could still suffer a horrible death at that temperature and the Met Office is advising people to keep their heads and the back of their necks covered, just to be on the safe side.

'Through the Tombstone'
with
Bartimaeus Grossman

Before I even enter today's tomb, we can see from the garden surrounding the entrance that whoever lies here was quite important. We can tell this by the fact that there are two temple guards lying dazed outside the tomb - whoever is in here wanted to make sure they stayed in here. This can also be seen by the seal that was placed on the stone at the entrance. Although, the seal is now broken and, unusually for 'Through the Tombstone', the stone has already been moved, which saves me a job.

As we step inside the tomb, we can see straight away that this is the resting place of someone quite wealthy. The craftsmanship of the interior walls is of a very high standard. As, we move towards the plinth where the body should be, we can see more evidence of an important burial – there looks to be around seventy-five pounds of spices here. That sort of amount is usually reserved for the likes of royalty.

It is here, though, that any similarities to other tombs end. For as we move closer to the plinth, it becomes apparent to us that there is no body! We can see that the strips of linen used to wrap the body in are still lying there in the shape of the owner, but the spices are just sitting on top of them and the head cloth is neatly folded in the corner here. So whoever was in here either stopped being as dead as he had been or was stolen by some very tidy body snatchers.

So let's look at the evidence: the temple guards; the broken seal; the large amount of spices and the neatly folded face cloth. Who was dead in a tomb like this? David, it's over to you.

The Judean
Tourist Association

Mr. and Mrs. Sedgwick

30 Olive Tree Crescent

Gaza

Judea

JU12 6HK

Dear Mum and Dad,

Brilliant news!!! Jesus is back! Mary Magdalene went to his tomb but he wasn't there and then she saw some angels and then she saw him but she didn't know it was him but it was and then he came to see the rest of us and I've seen him and he's real and he ate my fish sandwich but I didn't mind 'cause he was probably hungry after being dead for three days and he showed us the holes in his hands – they were gross! Uncle Peter's a lot happier now!

Lots of love,
Tobias

Picture: *Grutters at work*

The Temple of God

Gift Voucher

20 Silver Coins

This voucher entitles the bearer to goods worth up to 20 silver coins bought from any stall at the temple market or from the temple gift shop.

Presented to ..Jacob ben Jabel, temple guard.............

On the occasion of .....making up a pack of lies about........

.....Jesus not rising from the dead.....

To: Thomas Didymus
An Upper Room
Jerusalem

Dear Mr. Didymus,

We at the JSDSSP would like to thank you for letting us know about the suspected ghost of Jesus of Nazareth. As you know, we are happy to follow up any alleged Supernatural Phenomena in order to determine its authenticity. We have spent nearly a week studying eyewitness reports and we believe that we are now in a position to give you a definitive conjecture as to the genuineness of this 'ghost'.

Now, according to you and your fellow disciples, Jesus 'appeared from nowhere' in the middle of a room that was locked from the inside. This is certainly indicative behaviour of a supernatural being – many ghosts are unable to move solid objects and are therefore compelled to move through walls in order to travel from room to room. This is not, however, the case with Jesus, as your companions go on to say that he requested food and was given a fish sandwich to eat. Now, if this was a typical ghost, the food would simply have fallen straight through his body onto the floor – but it didn't.

And this is not the only time that Jesus has handled food. According to two of your colleagues who met Jesus on the Road to Emmaus, he sat with them and broke bread. If this were a true ghost, Mr Didymus, he would not have been able to lift even a single crumb.

All the evidence so far suggests that your Jesus is a real person – not a ghost. How this could have happened when he was clearly dead as a doornail this time last week is not clear. The fact remains, though, that, although he does possess supernatural powers, he is as solid as you and me. You were right to doubt, though, Mr. Didymus. In my opinion, a sceptical mind is a very healthy thing, but in this case, I believe your doubts were unfounded.

There is one last test you could administer, however, if you're still not certain Jesus is alive. According to the reports, he still had the holes in his hands and feet from the nails, and also in his side from a Roman spear. Why not insist on sticking your hands in them just to be sure? I certainly wouldn't want to do it myself and you may have to put up with your mates thinking you're a bit of a sicko, but it will certainly be compelling evidence one way or the other.

Whatever you decide, Mr. Didymus, I wish you well.

Yours sincerely,

Thaddeus Ben Jeb
Director, JSDSSP

The Roman Empire

Making the world a better place

Simon Peter
Fisherman
Nazareth
Palestine

Department of Fisheries and Livestock
Floor 3a
Imperial Headquarters
Rome

Dear Mr. Peter,

It has come to the attention of this department that you and your brother Andrew have contravened Rule 317 of the Roman Fishing and Farming Act of 23 BC. Section 17, Paragraph iii of the ruling clearly states that no more than 51 fish may be caught by any one vessel per day – except on Mondays and the second and fourth Thursday of each month, when the quota is raised to 54 fish.

We have reports that you and your brother exceeded this quota on the morning of Wednesday, May 28th. And not just by a little bit. We have reason to believe that your catch exceeded 150 large fish! Furthermore, we know that this was not the first time such a violation has taken place. We have record of a written warning sent to you three years ago by this department for the very same misdemeanour.

Now, I do like to think of myself as a fair man, Mr. Peter. The Roman Empire is not, after all, a ruthless autocracy run by self-serving politicians and power-crazed despots. At least, that is not how we would have you view us. I have, therefore, decided to give you one more chance. If you agree never again to exceed your fishing quota, you will not hear from this department again.

The Roman Empire is built on law and order, Mr Peter, and it will not tolerate anything out of the ordinary. As long as you keep your head down from now on and do nothing to attract attention to yourselves, no harm will come to you. Good day.

Yours,

L. Isaacs

Director, Department of Fisheries and Livestock

UFO MONTHLY

Issue 62, June

Jesus of Nazareth is an alien!

Well, we at UFO Monthly have been saying it for three years now and we have finally been proved right! Jesus of Nazareth, the popular preacher and healer who spent three years wandering around Judea and Galilee performing 'miracles', was last week seen returning to his mother ship. This is despite being crucified and buried at the Passover Feast six weeks ago!

He and his loyal band of followers travelled to Bethany and waited for the mother ship to arrive. Jesus gave some last-minute instructions to his followers and then held up his hands to the sky – presumably to signal that he was ready. Then he rose slowly into the sky, hovered about 20 feet above the ground for a second and vanished.

We first suspected Jesus was an alien three years ago. Issue 31 was the first to feature him when he began to heal the sick. Since then there has rarely been a UFO Monthly that hasn't featured Jesus for some reason or another.

This last proof of Jesus' true identity is a bittersweet success for us, however. For the editorial staff of this esteemed magazine have grown very fond of Jesus over the last few months and, if this truly is the end of his time here on earth, we will be very sad to see him go. We only hope that the report he gives about Planet Earth will be a good one and that he won't hold the whole crucifixion and burial thing against us.

And so, Jesus, from all the staff at UFO Monthly and our loyal band of readers, we bid you 'Farewell, good trip, live long and prosper, nanu nanu!'

FULL STORY AND PICTURES INSIDE!

Also in this issue…

An alien ate my camel!
We investigate the curious disappearance of Benjamin Betzold's prize camel, Frederick.

It's a Martian Conspiracy!
We ask, 'Why *does* bread always land butter-side down?'

Pull-Out Alien Poster!
A fantastic picture of the Sanhedrin's secret pod nursery!

Free Model!
Make your own replica of Jesus' mother ship! Full plans and specifications included. (Note: based entirely on editor's imagination.)

The Followers of Jesus Christ – Weekly Meeting
- Minutes -

Leader: Simon Peter
Secretary: Luke the Physician
Date: Sunday, 21st June

The meeting was held in the Upper Room. It began at the 2nd hour.

Apologies for Absence: None

Agenda: Minutes of last meeting
Find a replacement for Judas
AOB

Minutes of the last meeting were read and agreed.

Peter opened the main meeting by announcing that it was God's will that a replacement should be found for Judas Iscariot, on account of his being a betraying snake who let Jesus and all of his friends down - and also because his intestines were splattered all over some field outside of Jerusalem.
The motion was seconded by John and was passed by unanimous vote.

It was agreed that the replacement should have been with the disciples during the whole time that Jesus was active – from John's baptism until he ascended into heaven.
Two candidates were proposed: Joseph, also known as Barsabbas,

also known as Justus.

Matthias

After much prayer and the casting of lots, Matthias was chosen to take Judas's place, which is just as well because no one could remember which name to call the other one.

After much hugging and hand shaking, the meeting was resumed.

Bartholomew wanted to know when the apostles were going to get around to decorating the Upper Room, as he felt it was a bit dingy and could do with a touch of paint. It was agreed that Bart should go and buy some Magnolia paint tomorrow and get some of the lads to help him with the work.

Simon the Zealot wanted to know when we were going to go out and beat up some Romans in Jesus' name. It was agreed that this was probably a bad idea, as Jesus had expressly forbidden us to go anywhere until he sent his Holy Spirit. Simon felt that this was just an excuse because we were all a bunch of pansies. Peter was about to lay hands on Simon when Mary brought in a steaming pot of stew.

There was no other business after this and the meeting ended at ten to the 3rd hour.

Minutes written up by Luke the Physician

The Followers of Jesus Christ – Weekly Meeting
- Minutes -

Leader: Simon Peter
Secretary: Luke the Physician
Date: Sunday, 28th June

The meeting was held in the Upper Room. It began at the 2nd hour.

Apologies for Absence: None

Agenda: Minutes of last meeting
AOB

Minutes of the last meeting were read and agreed.

Peter opened the meeting by complimenting Bartholomew on the decorating work. It was unanimously agreed that the Upper Room looked much more cheerful now.

Matthew respectfully enquired if anyone knew where his mug was, as it was a gift from his Uncle Jonah and therefore had some sentimental value. The cup was found by Thaddeus, who had mistakenly put it with his things.

Simon the Zealot suggested once again that it might be a good idea to go out and break a few Roman soldiers before he felt compelled to break one of his fellow disciples' noses. Again, the motion was unanimously rejected and Simon was taken out of the meeting to calm down and have a nice cup of Mary's tea.

There was no other business after this and the meeting ended at quarter past the 2nd hour.

Minutes written up by Luke the Physician

The Followers of Jesus Christ – Weekly Meeting
- Minutes -

Leader: Simon Peter
Secretary: Luke the Physician
Date: Sunday, 5th July

The meeting was held in the Upper Room. It began at the 2nd hour.

Apologies for Absence: Simon the Zealot

Agenda: Minutes of last meeting
AOB

Minutes of the last meeting were read and agreed.

Peter opened the meeting by suggesting that there may not be any point in having a meeting, as nothing had happened for a long time now and there wasn't anything to discuss. He then suggested we all went out and enjoyed the Pentecost celebrations.

Simon the Zealot, who was supposed to be absent from the meeting on the suggestion of some of the apostles, fought his way into the room and demanded that he was allowed to go and beat up at least one Roman soldier.

A discussion on this subject was about to break out when a strange noise began to move around the room, like a strong wind. Suddenly, a large tongue of fire appeared in the middle of the room. It split into smaller tongues and rested on the heads of everyone present. As this happened, each one of us began to speak in different languages. Everyone ran out of the house and began to preach the good news of Jesus to the crowds - each person hearing them in their own language!

There was no other business after this and the meeting ended at ten past the 2nd hour.

Minutes written up by Luke the Physician

Dear All,

Well, it's been another big year for heaven and mankind alike. What with the feeding of the 5000 and dusting Moses and Elijah off for the transfiguration, raising Lazarus from the dead and, of course, the crucifixion and resurrection. Never let it be said that I don't do miracles like I used to.

So that's it – mission accomplished. Mankind can once again have a relationship with me. Boy, does that feel good! But that's not the end of the story. We're going to be busier than ever from here on in. Now that my Spirit is on the loose down there, there's no telling what could happen. It's going to be fun, though. I hope you angels are up for it. Just a few more centuries to go and before you know it, it'll be time for the Last Judgement – now *that's* going to be a day to remember!

See you there!

Bible References